FERRARI
THE ROAD CARS

The pre-war Scuderia Ferrari team Alfa Romeos were the first cars to carry the now world-famous Cavallino Rampante shields on their bonnets.

FERRARI
THE ROAD CARS

KEITH BLUEMEL

SUTTON PUBLISHING LIMITED

First published in the United Kingdom in 1998 by
Sutton Publishing Limited · Phoenix Mill · Thrupp · Stroud
Gloucestershire GL5 2BU

Revised paperback edition first published in 2000

A catalogue record for this book is available from the British Library

Photographic Credits

Period black and white static/studio courtesy Pininfarina, Bertone and Vignale. Period
black and white action courtesy of Ferret Photographics. Colour courtesy of Marcel
Massini, Jamie White and myself.

I am also grateful to Jonathan Flower for his help.

ISBN 0 7509 2483 7..

ᵀᴹ ALAN SUTTONᵀᴹ and SUTTONᵀᴹ are the
trade marks of Sutton Publishing Limited

Typeset in 11/15 Baskerville.
Typesetting and origination by
Sutton Publishing Limited.
Printed in Hong Kong by
Midas Printing Limited.

CONTENTS

The Formula 1-based engine of the F50.

CHRONOLOGY

1898   18 February, Enzo Ferrari born; birth registered 20 February

1919   5 October, Enzo Ferrari enters first motor race in a CMN

1920   Enzo Ferrari becomes a member of the Alfa Romeo racing team

1923   28 April, Enzo Ferrari marries Laura Garello, and Countess Baracca reportedly presents Enzo Ferrari with the Cavallino Rampante emblem

1928   King Victor Emmanuel III bestows honorary title Commendatore on Enzo Ferrari

1929   Scuderia Ferrari formed; registered on 29 November

1932   28 April, Dino Ferrari born

1938   Alfa Romeo cease supporting Scuderia Ferrari and take the racing department back to Milan under the title Alfa Corse

1939   Enzo Ferrari parts company with Alfa Romeo and forms Auto Avio Costruzione

1940   Two Auto Avio Costruzione 815 cars produced

1945   22 May, son Piero born of Lina Lardi, and Gioacchino Colombo starts design work on the first Ferrari V12 engine

1946   Auto Avio Costruzione changes name to Auto Costruzione Ferrari

1947   First Ferrari car produced, the type 125; it is victorious in its second race, the Rome Grand Prix on 25 May

1948   Biondetti/Navone win the Mille Miglia in a Ferrari 166 Allemano-bodied coupé. Ferrari displays two cars at the Turin Salon for the first time

1949   Chinetti/Selsdon win the first postwar Le Mans 24 Hour Race in a 166MM barchetta. Two weeks later Chinetti/Lucas win the Spa 24 Hour Race in a similar car. Biondetti/Salani win the Mille Miglia in a 166MM barchetta

1950   Inauguration of the Formula 1 Drivers' World Championship. Marzotto/Crosara win the Mille Miglia in a 195 Touring berlinetta

1951   Froilan Gonzalez gives Ferrari their first victory in the Formula 1 World Championship, winning the British Grand Prix at Silverstone. Villoresi/Cassani win the Mille Miglia in a 340 America Vignale berlinetta

1952   Alberto Ascari wins the Formula 1 World Championship in a Ferrari; the Mille Miglia is won by Bracco/Rolfo in a 250 Sport Vignale berlinetta. Ferrari win the Manufacturers' Championship

1953   Albert Ascari takes second in the Formula 1 World Championship title in a Ferrari; G. Marzotto/Crosara repeat their 1950 victory in the Mille Miglia, this time in a 340MM Vignale spider. Ferrari win the Manufacturers' Championship

1954   Gonzales/Trintignant win the Le Mans 24 Hour Race in a 375 Plus. Ferrari win the Manufacturers' Championship

1956   30 June, Dino Ferrari dies. Juan Manuel Fangio wins the Formula 1 World Championship in a Ferrari, while in the Mille Miglia Ferraris fill the top five places, Castellotti winning in a

290MM. Ferrari win the Manufacturers' Championship

1957 Taruffi wins the last Mille Miglia in a 315S; The fatal crash of De Portago involving spectators caused the cessation of the event. Ferrari win the Manufacturers' Championship

1958 Mike Hawthorn wins the Formula 1 World Championship in a Ferrari, and P. Hill/Gendebien in a 250 Testa Rossa win the Le Mans 24 Hour Race. Ferrari win the Manufacturers' Championship

1960 Name of company is changed to Societa Esercizio Fabbriche Automobili e Corse Ferrari, or SEFAC Ferrari for short. Gendebien/Frere in a 250TRI win the Le Mans 24 Hour Race. Ferrari win the Manufacturers' Championship

1961 Phil Hill becomes the first American Formula 1 World Champion in a Ferrari, with Ferrari taking the Formula 1 Constructors' Championship. The Hill/Gendebien duo in a 250TRI repeat their 1958 victory in the Le Mans 24 Hour Race. Ferrari win the Manufacturers' Championship

1962 Hill/Gendebien reach their joint hat trick of Le Mans victories. Ferrari win the Manufacturers' Championship

1963 Bandini/Scarfiotti in a 250P win the Le Mans 24 Hour Race. Ferrari win the Manufacturers' Championship

1964 John Surtees becomes the first person to be World Champion on both a motorcycle and in a car, driving a Ferrari, with Ferrari taking the Formula 1 Constructors' Championship. The 275P of Guichet/Vacarella wins the Le Mans 24 Hour Race. Ferrari win the Manufacturers' Championship

1965 Rindt/Gregory win the Le Mans 24 Hour Race in a 275LM. Ferrari win the Manufacturers' Championship. Ferrari and Fiat sign an agreement for the latter to produce the V6 Dino engine for use by both companies

1967 Ferrari score a memorable 1-2-3 victory in the Daytona 24 Hour Race, that results in the unofficial adoption of the title 'Daytona' for the 365GTB/4 road car. Ferrari win the Manufacturers' Championship

1969 Fiat purchase 40 per cent of Ferrari share capital, with a further 49 per cent going to them upon the death of Enzo Ferrari, who retains full control over the racing department

1972 Ferrari win the Manufacturers' Championship. Fiorano test track opened adjacent to the factory in Maranello

1975 Niki Lauda wins Formula 1 World Championship in a Ferrari, with Ferrari taking the Formula 1 Constructors' Championship

1976 Ferrari win the Formula 1 Constructors' Championship

1977 Niki Lauda wins his second Formula 1 World Championship in a Ferrari, with Ferrari again taking the Formula 1 Constructors' Championship

1979 Jody Scheckter wins the Formula 1 World Championship in a Ferrari, with Ferrari taking the Formula 1 Constructors' Championship

1982 Ferrari win the Formula 1 Constructors' Championship, and a new competition department is built next to the Fiorano circuit

1983 Ferrari win the Formula 1 Constructors' Championship

1988 February, Enzo Ferrari celebrates his ninetieth birthday, hosting a party in the factory for the entire staff. 4 June, Pope John Paul II visits the Ferrari factory. 14 August, Enzo Ferrari dies. Ferrari purchase Mugello race circuit near Florence

1989 Company name changes from SEFAC Ferrari to Ferrari SpA

1995 November, Ferrari open a website on the Internet, address is http://www.ferrari.it

1997 Ferrari acquires 50 per cent of Maserati SpA

INTRODUCTION

The Ferrari story began in Modena, Italy, on 18 February 1898 when Adalgisa Ferrari, wife of Alfredo, gave birth to their second son. Because of heavy snowfall it was two days before his birth could be registered, the name on the certificate reading Enzo Anselmo Ferrari. This was the beginning of a life that would lead to a fairly common Italian name becoming one of the most famous in the automobile world and beyond.

In his youth Enzo Ferrari had three ambitions: to be an operatic tenor, a sports writer and a racing driver. The first was only a fantasy as he didn't have the voice; the second he achieved briefly in his teenage years, when his report on a football match was published in the national newspaper *Gazzetto dello Sport*. His skill with the pen never left him and in later years he wrote various books, mainly autobiographical, which he usually published privately. The third ambition, to be a racing driver, he realized shortly after he completed his military service, and he continued with some degree of success, including a second place in the 1920 Targa Florio, until he gave up competition on the birth of his son Dino in 1932.

In 1920 another event occured which was to become part of the Ferrari legend when, after winning a race at Ravenna, he met Count Baracca, the father of a First World War fighter pilot killed in the conflict. He was subsequently introduced to the Countess, who perhaps saw in him a kindred spirit with her deceased son, and asked him to carry her son's 'Cavallino Rampante' emblem on his racing cars for luck. He agreed to this and placed the rearing black stallion design on a yellow background, the colour of the town of his birth. The original Baracca stallion had a drooping tail, which Ferrari amended to an erect tail, perhaps feeling that it created a more positive image. This badge has seen small detail changes over the years, mainly the slimming of the body shape in keeping with the image of the cars that it adorns, and, like the name of the founder, has become one of the most widely known and easily recognized company logos in the world.

Before Dino's birth Enzo Ferrari had set up an Alfa Romeo dealership on the Viale Trento e Trieste in Modena which he called Scuderia Ferrari. This was the official sales and service centre for the Emilia Romagna region. When Enzo gave up racing himself Scuderia Ferrari became the official racing division of Alfa Romeo, and instead of the '*Quadrifoglio*' (four-leaf clover) emblem on the bonnet sides the cars carried the Cavallino Rampante on a yellow shield. One of the team's star drivers

The Cavallino Rampante appears in many guises, here seen across the rear of an F40 at the entrance to the Ferrari-owned Cavallino restaurant, which is opposite the main factory gates in Maranello.

This bronze Cavallino Rampante graces the portico of the entrance door to the house in the centre of the Fiorano circuit, close to the factory. This house was frequently used by Enzo Ferrari.

was the legendary Tazio Nuvolari, whom Ferrari held in higher esteem than virtually anybody else who ever drove for him. In 1938 Alfa Romeo decided to bring its racing activities back 'in house', under the title of Alfa Corse and with Enzo Ferrari as a director. The lack of freedom in his new role resulted in Ferrari departing in 1939, the terms of severance preventing him from producing a car bearing his name for a period of four years.

Immediately he formed a new company, Auto Avio Costruzione, and work started on producing their first car. This was constructed on a modified Fiat chassis and was powered by a straight-eight 1.5-litre engine, developed from two four-cylinder Fiat engines with a light aluminium body designed and built by Touring of Milan. It carried a small badge on the nose with only the inscription '815' on it which referred to the number of cylinders and cubic capacity

of the engine, a feature that would recur occasionally in Ferrari model designations. Two examples were built and entered in the 1940 Mille Miglia although neither finished, Ferrari had started car production, albeit under an alias. The Mille Miglia, along with the Targa Florio, was a very important road race in Italy for car manufacturers. They were both gruelling tests of speed and reliability and a win ensured enormous publicity. The Mille Miglia was a 1,000-mile non-stop road race from Brescia to Rome and back, and the Targa Florio a road race through the mountains and villages of Sicily, covering a variety of routes over the years.

The Second World War curtailed any further automobile production work for the duration of the conflict, and the AAC operation was moved out of Modena to the small town of Maranello at the foot of the Appenines. This new factory, with a staff of about a hundred during the war years, initially produced aero engines for training aircraft and then copies of German machine tools, such as lathes and milling machines. It is perhaps worth mentioning that even the machinery sales catalogues carried the Cavallino Rampante emblem. At the end of the war the machine tool production was wound down as thoughts of car manufacturing were rekindled, this time without having to construct a façade as the contractual obligation to Alfa Romeo had long since expired.

Before the war Ferrari had worked with an engineer by the name of Gioacchino Colombo at Alfa Romeo on the 158 Alfetta. Now the war was over Colombo was looking for a new challenge and Ferrari commissioned him to design a V12 engine for his proposed new car. It is alleged that Ferrari's passion for the V12 concept had evolved from a photograph that he had seen when he was young of the 1914 Packard V12 Indianapolis car. No time was lost in turning Colombo's drawings into metal and in March 1947 the first car to bear the name Ferrari came out of the Maranello works. This was given the model designation '125', which referred to the swept volume of each cylinder, hence the total cubic capacity was 1500cc. Again, this was to be a method of model designation frequently used by Ferrari over the following years.

The first car constructed by Ferrari was the Auto Avio Costruzione 815, with a 1.5-litre straight-eight engine and an aluminium body by Carrozzeria Touring, built in 1940. Two examples were made and were raced in the 1940 Mille Miglia but both retired. Then the Second World War brought a halt to car construction and racing for the company. The car pictured is chassis number 021, the sole surviving example, the other having been recorded as scrapped many years ago.

The new Ferrari had its maiden race at Piacenza in the hands of Franco Cortese, where it retired while in the lead. The Rome Grand Prix on 25 May 1947 saw Cortese take the 125 to victory in only its second race. By the end of the year the tally was fourteen starts, seven wins and four second places. The 125 was succeeded in 1948 by the 2-litre 166 model in which Biondetti took victory in the prestigious Mille Miglia, the year ending with competition in twenty-eight races, netting ten wins, eleven second and six third places. The 166 series continued into 1949 with the introduction of the 'Mille Miglia' models, named in honour of Biondetti's victory. These carried both open and closed aluminium bodywork by Carrozzeria Touring, the open version being dubbed 'barchetta' ('little boat') because of the way the coachwork curved under along its base, reminiscent of a speedboat. This year also saw Ferrari achieve worldwide recognition when the Chinetti/Selsdon partnership won the Le Mans 24 Hour Race in a 166MM barchetta. Luigi Chinetti partnered by Jean Lucas followed with a further victory in the Spa 24 Hour Race two weeks later. This model also spawned the development of limited production high-performance road cars for wealthy clients, necessary to finance the competition activity. In fact Enzo Ferrari was often quoted as saying that he only produced road cars to pay the bills of the racing team.

In 1950 the Formula 1 World Drivers' Championship was inaugurated and Ferrari cars are the only ones to have participated from its inception to the present day. Their first victory in the series came on 14 July 1951 when Froilan Gonzalez took a 375 Formula 1 to victory in the British Grand Prix at Silverstone. Since then Ferraris have won more than a hundred Grand Prix, gaining nine drivers' and eight constructors' championships along the way. The success on the racetrack wasn't only confined to single seaters, as from the late 1940s to the early '70s there were numerous successes in Sports and GT races. These included eight Le Mans victories, six of these being consecutive between 1960 and '65; eight Mille Miglia wins; seven in the Targa Florio; and a clean sweep in the Tour de France Auto every year between 1956 and 1965. There were also inevitable tragedies along the way, but none more so than for Enzo Ferrari when his son Dino died after years of ill health on 30 June 1956. After this Enzo became more reclusive and rarely left the confines of the Modena–Maranello corridor.

In the early 1950s Ferrari produced a bewildering number of road and competition models, with a variety of engine sizes and configurations, and coachwork by many of the leading Italian *carrozzeria*, including Touring, Vignale, Ghia and Pinin Farina. A 212 model was even bodied by the British company Abbott, but was not considered attractive, and no longer exists in this form. The models produced during this period were all very small series production and most cars had individual differences, even if ostensibly they appeared the same. It was not until 1955 that some semblance of series production evolved with the announcement of the Pinin Farina-designed 250 Europa GT. From this time Pinin Farina, to become Pininfarina in 1958, virtually became the exclusive coachwork designer for Ferrari, with very few exceptions. The only deviation of note, in volume terms, was the Dino 308GT4 that came from the pen of Bertone.

Even though a more standardized production-line technique came to be adopted there was still scope within the

Sergio Pininfarina, head of the Turin-based company whose name has been synonymous with the design of Ferrari coachwork since the mid-1950s.

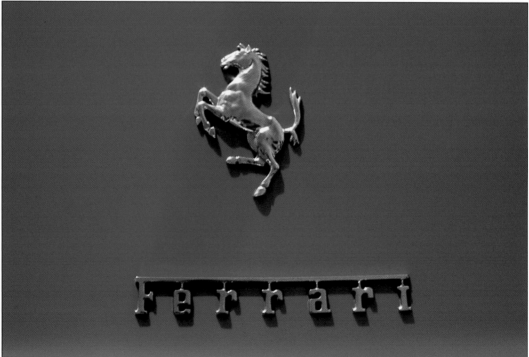

The Cavallino Rampante in chrome together with the Ferrari logo featuring the familiar elongated 'F', seen here on the bootlid of a 275GTB. Both trademarks are vigorously guarded by the factory against unauthorized use.

structure to produce specialized one-off, or very limited run, models right up to the late 1960s. This philosophy was resurrected in the mid-1980s with the 288 GTO, followed by the F40 in 1987 and then the F50. However, in comparison with the early years, even the 288 GTO, with 272 units made, was mass produced. The mainstream of Ferrari road-car production from the mid-1950s to the mid-1960s was a development of the 250GT series. These were replaced by the 275GT and 330GT models, which ran to the late 1960s before being replaced by the 365GT series, which included the 1970s' last front-engined 'Supercar', the 365GTB/4 Daytona. The mid-engined Dino introduced as a separate marque, with its own badge created from Dino Ferrari's signature, pointed the way forward for future mainstream production, with the engine to the rear of the passenger compartment. Only the large capacity four-seater models would remain front engined until their demise in 1989 and revival in 1992 with the 456GT. The return to a front-engine format for a two-seater model occured in 1996 with the announcement of the 550 Maranello; time will tell if the smaller capacity models follow suit.

In the early years many of the models were truly dual purpose road and competition cars and even today many of the sports racing models of the 1950s see road use at historic events. Whether a car is classified as a road vehicle or as purely a competition machine is a grey area. For the purposes of this book I have taken the late 1950s for the open sports racing models, and the mid-1960s for the closed competition GT cars as the end of the periods when I consider that competition cars could be feasibly used on the road, albeit with a couple of exceptions which will be highlighted.

In the mid-1960s Ford tried unsuccessfully to purchase Ferrari and, when their negotiations failed, they entered motor sport on their own account with the renowned GT40, having provided finance for the Ford-engined AC Cobra project. This produced some of the most enthralling endurance races ever witnessed, as David (Ferrari) tried to fend off Goliath (Ford). The financial toll of competition, allied with the increasingly complex and expensive regulations governing the sport, brought about the marriage of Ferrari with Fiat in 1969, by which time there were nearly 1,000 people on the payroll at Ferrari. Fiat acquired a 40 per cent share in Ferrari, although Enzo Ferrari retained control of the competition department and his second son Piero retained 10 per cent of the main company. By 1969 Enzo Ferrari was already seventy years old and probably viewed the deal as a means of ensuring the longevity of the company bearing his name.

In February 1988 Enzo Ferrari celebrated his ninetieth birthday with a huge party in the factory for all the staff, now numbering over 1,700, and in the same month was awarded an honorary degree in physics by the University of Modena. On 4 June Pope John Paul II visited the Maranello factory but Enzo Ferrari was too ill to attend, although the two men spoke by telephone. His health continued to deteriorate and on 14 August 1988 the man whose name had become the most famous in the annals of motoring history passed away.

Fortunately, the foundations he laid, the decisions he made and the mystique and aura that he created have placed Ferrari in a unique position in motoring history, with a popularity that transcends national barriers and unites all aficionados of the cars bearing the Cavallino Rampante.

The founder of the Ferrari marque, Enzo Ferrari, is seen here in Modena in 1987 at eighty-nine years of age.

A production line at the Ferrari factory in the late 1980s, with a Mondial coupé nearing completion in the foreground.

Chapter 1

THE EARLY YEARS

The first car to be produced bearing the Ferrari badge was the 125, with a 1500cc V12 engine. The model number referred to the cubic capacity of one cylinder, which was a familiar practice for many years with Ferrari. A model of this type gave Ferrari their first race victory in May 1947 when Franco Cortese won the Rome Grand Prix. These cars were upgraded to 159 and 166 models but none of the original cars survive. This example is a Ferrari-built reproduction of the original model, carrying chassis number 90125.

Introduction

In 1947, Enzo Ferrari's first year manufacturing cars under his own name, three cars were produced according to official figures from the Ferrari factory. These were called the type 125, although they were subsequently upgraded and modified into the type 159S and 166 models. None of these three cars exist in their original form and opinions differ among Ferrari historians as to which of the 166 models surviving today can lay claim to being the oldest surviving Ferrari. Ferrari started construction of a new fully operational 125 model in 1987, exactly as the original drawings, and gave it a chassis number in the production model range of 90125; 90 for 1990, the year that it was fully completed, and 125 for the model type. Since then this example has been exhibited at Ferrari gatherings around the world.

In 1948 the factory records show five cars were produced and included a spider, a designation originally given to an open sports body, and a coupé, fixed roof design, both bodied by Allemano. These were produced together with the Turin Salon cars bodied by Touring to the *superleggera* ('super lightweight') principles of their chief designer, Felice Bianchi Anderloni, which were a 166 Sport coupé and a 166MM barchetta. This latter body style was one of the most popular designs of the period and, apart from clothing the 166MM, it was also used for 195, 212, 225 and 340 models, together with a berlinetta derivative, up to 1952. The berlinetta description was generally used to designate a closed fastback competition model. Almost from the start the practice of providing road cars with odd chassis numbers and competition sports cars with even chassis numbers was introduced. This practice continued up to chassis number 75000, when it was abandoned, road cars being provided with a continuous numerical sequence and competition sports cars, like the F333SP sports prototype, getting their own model range chassis-number sequence. The single-seater formula cars have their own unrelated chassis-number sequences.

In 1949 Stablimenti Farina, not to be confused with Pinin Farina, provided coupé and cabriolet examples of the 166 Inter model, while the 166MM barchetta provided the production backbone and put the Ferrari name firmly on the international map, with wins in the Mille Miglia and at the Le Mans and Spa 24 Hour races. The success of the 166MM barchetta saw the previous year's production figure quadruple, with twenty-one cars manufactured in this year.

The start of a new decade saw the number of coachbuilders clothing Ferrari chassis increase dramatically, with examples from Bertone, Ghia, Motto, Reggiani and Vignale joining those of Farina and Touring during 1950. It was to be the work of Touring and Vignale that would prove to be the most desirable to the clientele during the early 1950s. It can be very difficult to determine exactly what a particular model is, not only for the uninitiated, but also for those with a knowledge of the subject – for example, the barchetta body by Touring clothed five different models. Although they don't all have the same wheelbase and thus the body proportions are different, to the casual observer they are virtually identical.

To add to the confusion of what a particular model may be is the fact that some cars were rebodied during the period just after their construction with a different body to the original. This was sometimes done after an accident or perhaps when the owner wanted a change and it was cheaper to commission a new body than to purchase a completely new car. It is important to remember that from the start a Ferrari was not a cheap car to purchase. In June 1951 the magazine *Autocar* quoted a price of approximately £3,200 for a Ferrari 212 barchetta, nearly three times the price of a Jaguar XK 120, with an Austin A40 saloon costing just over £500.

With familiarization the styling cues of different coachbuilders becomes evident, such as the 'portholes' on the front wings which were typical of Vignale from this period. Most coachbuilders also added their own badge to publicize their creation but it is still difficult to find anything to positively identify a particular model.

In 1951 a further name appeared on the Ferrari coachbuilder's role of honour, a name that in later years was to become synonymous with the design of Ferrari bodywork – this was of course Pinin Farina. Their first efforts were made on the 212 Inter model, for which they produced coupé and cabriolet variants. Although their creations were less flamboyant than some of their contemporaries, they were elegant and must have struck a chord with Enzo Ferrari.

During 1952 and '53 the styling houses already mentioned continued to clothe the Ferrari chassis, with a gradual swing towards the work of Pinin Farina, although the designs of Vignale continued to prove popular, particularly for the competition spiders. With the 250MM and 340MM models there was a choice of a Pinin Farina berlinetta or a Vignale spider. The Vignale spider was available with two completely different body styles, one of which was also fitted to the 166MM/53 model, thus making identification even more difficult.

This period in Ferrari history is perhaps the most difficult to understand owing to the wide diversity of engines, chassis, and the myriad of bodies used to clothe them. However, it is also very rewarding because of the sheer spectrum of models produced by what was then only a fledgling company.

The 166 spider Corsa of 1948 was a development of the 125, with a two-seater cycle wing body and a two-litre V12 engine. The car seen here is chassis number 002C, which vies with 166 spider Corsa chassis number 010I/01C as the earliest surviving Ferrari according to automobile historians. This is likely to remain an insoluble question as the chassis were renumbered and modified to suit contemporary circumstances, with thought only for the present and, not for any possible future historical record.

The 166 spider Corsa engine of chassis number 010I/01C. Seen here is the plain camshaft cover of the left bank of cylinders, the triple carburettors in the centre of the vee, the siamesed exhaust manifolds and magnettos driven off the end of each camshaft disappearing into cutouts in the bulkhead.

The 166MM Touring barchetta ('little boat'), so named because of the way the body curved under along the sides, was produced between 1948 and 1950. Some of these were later upgraded to 195 specification by providing a longer stroke, giving an engine capacity of 2341cc. There were sometimes individual differences in the radiator grille shape and other small body details but the general configuration of all examples was basically the same, as can be seen from chassis numbers 0040M above, and 0064M below.

The engine of a 166MM. On this example the triple twin-choke carburettors feature short velocity stacks. The differences between this and the earlier 166 engine can be clearly seen – the camshaft cover is now cast to incorporate the Ferrari script, the magnettos are vertically mounted at the rear of the engine and the oil breathers are in a central position.

This 166 Inter coupé with Touring bodywork was produced in 1948 on chassis number 005S. It was shown alongside a 166MM barchetta at the 1948 Turin Salon, which marked Ferrari's debut as a manufacturer at an international motor show. The Carrozzeria Touring family resemblance can be seen in the front panel shape, although the overall design is clearly a pure road car.

In 1949–50 Stablimenti Farina produced five coupés and three cabriolets on the 166 Inter chassis. All carried very similar bodywork and individual differences related mainly to the radiator grille details, bumper configuration, small changes to lighting and disc or wire wheels.

Vignale's interpretation of coachwork on the 166 Inter coupé theme in 1950. In comparison with the Stablimenti Farina style, it is more modern with the single-piece windscreen and generally has a lighter more sporting feel to the lines.

In 1950 this unique Reggiani-designed coupé, nicknamed 'Uovo' ('Egg'), was built for the Marzotto brothers on 166MM chassis number 024MB, with the V12 engine rebuilt to 212 specification, i.e., a capacity of 2.56 litres, specifically to compete in the Mille Miglia road race. Apart from its unusual appearance, its main design feature was a lack of windscreen pillars, the screen being clamped between the bulkhead and the roof by tensioned steel wires.

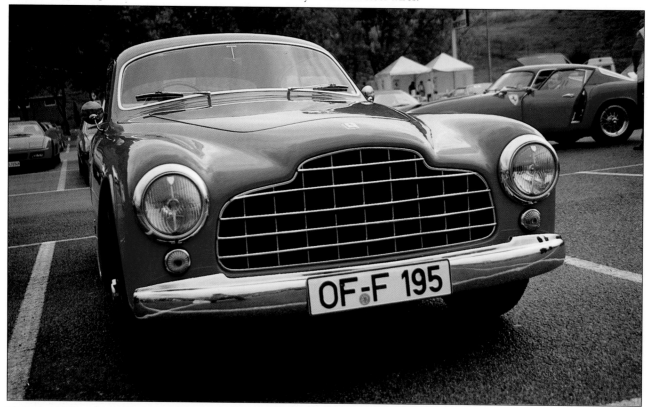

With the 166 engine gaining extra cubic capacity in 1950 to become the 195 model of 2341cc, the range of body designs on Ferrari chassis continued to expand. This is an example of a 195 Inter coupé produced by Ghia during 1950–1, which is quite similar to the earlier Stablimenti Farina offering in overall shape, albeit with a single-piece windscreen.

The 195 Inter coupé by Vignale was the most flamboyant of the offerings with heavier use of chrome – note the radiator grille and surround, together with the teardrop-shaped engine bay exhaust outlet on the wing. Also, the rear lights were frequently recessed into the wings with chrome sleeves to the recess on a number of Vignale offerings. Between 1950 and '54 Vignale produced a truly eclectic array of bodywork designs on numerous sport and road Ferraris.

This successful yet restrained design by Vignale started life as a rebody of a 166 Touring barchetta in 1952, but in later years the body was removed and fitted to a shortened 195 Inter chassis 097S. It now carries 195 Inter engine number 087S and must be considered something of a hybrid, although this doesn't detract from the elegant tight lines of the body.

The 1950 195S berlinetta with Touring bodywork has close family resemblances to the open 166MM barchetta, which was designed by the same company. This style of berlinetta body was also used on some 166MMs and in fact the 195S was basically a 166MM with the V12 engine bore increased to 65 mm, using the same 58.8 mm stroke, to give a capacity of 195.1cc per cylinder, hence the 195 model name, with an overall capacity of 2341cc. Some 166MMs had the bore increased to 195 specification to provide greater performance. The example seen here, chassis number 0060M, is generally believed to be the 1950 Mille Miglia winner in the hands of Marzotto/Crosara.

The badges of Ferrari and Carrozzeria Touring on the tail of a 166MM barchetta, the *superleggera* in the Touring badge refers to their 'superlight' construction method of small bore tubes to which the lightweight aluminium body was attached.

The engine bay of a 212, based on the original Colombo-designed V12, with a bore of 68 mm to provide a total engine capacity of 2.56 litres. There were two versions available: one was called the Inter, intended for road use with a single twin-choke carburettor, and the Export with triple twin-choke carburettors for competition. However, there was undoubtedly a crossover of specifications, dependent upon a client's wishes.

The 212 Export Touring barchetta produced in 1951–2 is very similar in appearance to the 166 and 195 examples that carry virtually identical bodywork from the Milanese *carrozzeria*. This example, chassis number 0136E, has driving lights, the forward part of the carburettor intake is sculpted into the bonnet and the windscreen is a split unit on a raised base. The American magazine *Road & Track* recorded a speed of 123.2mph over a flying quarter mile and a 0–60mph time of 7.05 seconds, which was very impressive for 1952.

In 1951 two 212 Exports were bodied by Motto, one a berlinetta on chassis number 0074E and the other a spider, seen here, on chassis number 0094E. The single central driving light in the bottom of the grille is an identifying feature, although this arrangement was also featured on a couple of Vignale-bodied Ferraris.

A 212 Export coupé by Vignale, chassis number 0111S, with a single central driving light in the grille. The nose of this car features a Ferrari badge on one side of the raised rib that extends from the grille along the bonnet and a Vignale one on the other side. The two-tone paint finish, with the lighter roof, draws the eye to the lower part of the body, particularly the large eggcrate grille.

A beautiful example of a 212 Export Vignale cabriolet, chassis number 0106E, which is obviously a road car but with an even competition chassis number which has been meticulously maintained by its long-time British owner. These views show the compact lines and Vignale's use of chrome to emphasize details, such as the aggressive stance the protruding central vertical bar gives to the radiator grille, the small grille on the bonnet for the carburettor air intake and the chromed reveals which pick out the recessed tail lights.

The frontal treatment of this 212 Inter Vignale coupé is quite similar to that used on the 212 Export cabriolet but doesn't feature the driving lights in the grille and the central vertical chrome bar is not as pronounced. However, at this time no two cars were identical and you could even find dimensional differences from one side of a car to the other. This particular car, chassis number 0163E, was sold new in Lisbon, Portugal, and the client requested this black with pale-green roof colour scheme, so that it would resemble the town's taxis, thus hoping to maintain a low profile.

This Vignale 212 Export, chassis number 0170ET, was upgraded by the factory to 225 engine size (2.7 litre) soon after it was built. This view shows off the very compact coupé body, with typical Vignale details evident: two-tone paintwork, ovoid portholes on the wing sides and the recessed tail lights with chromed sleeves.

The variations offered by Vignale on any particular chassis were extremely wide over a very short period of time. Here is another example of a 212 Inter coupé, chassis number 0197EL, nicknamed the 'bumble-bee' by its owner for obvious reasons! The headlights have moved into the large oval grille, while the very slim wing line extends forward and incorporates recessed side lights. Vignale's use of chrome and two-tone paint to emphasize the lines of a car is quite obvious on this example.

A more restrained approach by Vignale was used on this 212 Inter coupé, chassis number 0237EU, although the styling cues are still there, such as the chrome-rimmed portholes in the wing sides and the chromed vertical cooling intake grilles either side of the radiator opening.

Vignale took a more flamboyant approach with this 212 Inter coupé, chassis number 0257EU, as can be seen with the bulbous wings incorporating high level wrap-around bumperettes above the sidelights, and the chrome strip running the length of the body side continuing the line of the bumperettes. The picture has not been reproduced back to front, the car is right-hand drive, but the Cavallino Rampante on the grille is facing the wrong way!

After all the Vignale interpretations on the 212 theme the 1951–3 offering from Pinin Farina, seen here on chassis number 0275EU, exhibits simple elegance with no frills, although the wilder creations of Vignale were more popular with clients at the time. This body style continued to be developed and formed the styling basis for the 250 Europa, 375 America and 250 Europa GT beween 1953 and '55.

This interpretation of a 212 Inter by Vignale on chassis number 0287EU, built in 1953, has a definite competition stance, with the large radiator grille, long bonnet, low cabin line and lack of chrome adornment. In fact it is very similar to the treatment that had been used by Vignale for the 1952 'Carrera Panamericana' 340 Mexico models.

This 340 America berlinetta by Vignale, chassis number 0082A, was the winner of the 1951 Mille Miglia driven by Villoresi/Cassani. The 340 in the title refers to the cubic capacity of one cylinder in the Aurelio Lampredi-designed V12 engine, actually 341.8cc, to give a total capacity of 4.1 litres. These engines had the cylinder liners screwed into the cylinder head and are generally referred to as 'long block' because of their greater length over the original Colombo-designed smaller capacity V12 engines.

This 340 America berlinetta from 1951, chassis number 0122A, carries coachwork by Touring, although the radiator grille shape is not dissimilar to the Vignale example. Only two 340 engined examples of this model were produced but similar bodywork was used on the 166, 195 and 212 models.

Five examples of the 340 America with Touring barchetta bodies were built during 1951 and chassis number 0118A is seen here. Again, the similarity in lines with their smaller-engined cousins can be clearly seen. It can also be noted that the nose on this example does not run in a continuous curve from the top of the radiator grille into the bonnet but has a step in the flow and this feature also appears on some examples of the smaller engine capacity models. The Ferrari factory claimed this was the fastest sports car in the world upon its release, with a quoted top speed of 149mph.

A 340 America with a Vignale coupé body, chassis number 0174A, that features the raised central bonnet ridge favoured by Vignale on a number of occasions in the early 1950s. Not visible in this view are other typical Vignale features: horizontal teardrop exhaust vents on the wing sides, and tail lights recessed in the wings.

Ghia also tried their hand on the 340 America and produced five examples in 1952 and chassis number 0142A is shown here. Again, this is a car with a competition even chassis number but is clearly designed for road use.

A very functional and restrained Vignale spider design on the 340 America, chassis number 0140A. The main Vignale styling cue on this body is the recessed tail lights which are not evident in this picture. This particular car was exported new to the USA and has remained in American ownership ever since.

The 340 Mexico competition berlinetta of 1952, chassis number 0226A, styled by Vignale and of which three examples were built as well as a spider that is virtually this body without the roof section. These cars were built specifically to contest the gruelling 1952 Carrera Panamericana road race but were subsequently used in other events after their success in that event.

The 225 Sport model of 1952 with its 2.7-litre engine was produced by Vignale with both coupé and spider bodies. This is one of the coupé versions, on chassis number 0152EL, which was obviously intended for competition with the large quick-release aluminium filler cap protruding through the rear window. The typical Vignale portholes can be seen on the front wings, although the rear lights have a conventional mounting.

A single 225 Sport was bodied by Touring with their traditional barchetta-style body on chassis number 0166ED but with a slightly different rear wing line and tail treatment, closer to that used on their berlinettas and also found on their renderings on the 340 America.

This is the Vignale spider version of the 225 Sport which is very similar to the design used on the 340 America spider but with a few more Vignale styling cues: the chrome grilled vertical cooling slots on either side of the radiator grille and the ovoid portholes in the front wing sides. A similar body style was also used on one 250MM spider.

The 1953 166MM Series II, chassis number 0314M, is seen here with Vignale spider bodywork and was the final evolution of the 166MM model. Other variants were berlinetta and coupé models by Vignale and a pair of Autodromo spiders, an Abarth spider and a Pinin Farina berlinetta. This very rounded style of Vignale spider bodywork, with minimal front and rear overhangs, was very popular with clients during 1953 and was also used to clothe 250MM, 340MM and 625TF models. This makes differentiation between individual types very difficult and even though one can find numerous differences between one car and another none are specific to a particular model. The 166MM with its 2,200 mm wheelbase, which is 200 mm shorter than the 250MM and 300 mm shorter than a 340MM, is the 'baby' of the trio, but even this is not apparent unless you have examples of the other models to compare it with.

A British-owned 166MM Vignale spider, chassis number 0308M, competing at the Prescott hillclimb in 1968. This shows some of the small differences between one car and another of the same model, i.e., the windscreen arrangement and the headlights.

This 166 Inter, chassis number 039S, was originally a 1949 Touring coupé but was rebodied in 1953 by Vignale with this very smooth and unadorned coupé body. The car was originally fitted with disc wheels but these have been replaced with wire wheels in recent years which complement the competition-orientated body style better.

This 342 model was the first competition-bodied Ferrari produced by Pinin Farina, chassis number 0236MM, and was the forerunner to their 250MM, 340MM and 375MM series of berlinettas which carried very similar bodywork in light aluminium. The 342 referred to the cubic capacity of one cylinder in the V12 engine, actually 341.8cc, which provided a total displacement of 4.1 litres. The same engine was used in the 340 models, with the designation change probably being made in the interests of simplicity.

The rear view of the 250MM is dominated by the large wrap-around perspex screen, with the large aluminium racing filler cap just below it. From any angle the lines are very smooth and clean, yet exude an air of purpose.

The 250MM Pinin Farina berlinetta can clearly be seen to be closely related to the 342 berlinetta in almost every detail. The raised sections on the rear wings are to provide additional clearance for the tyres but also help to cool them at the same time as they are open at the front and rear. The engine of this model was derived from the original Colombo-designed short block V12 unit, with a total cubic capacity of 3 litres, and was usually fitted with triple four-barrel Weber carburettors in these cars. In the picture below a 250MM Pinin Farina berlinetta, chassis number 0298MM, is seen competing in a historic race on the Monaco Grand Prix circuit in May 1997.

A 250MM berlinetta, chassis number 0258MM, competing in the 1953 Pescara 12 Hour Race. Note that this example has been provided with a carburettor intake in the bonnet.

The engine bay of a 250MM showing how it is dominated by the bank of three quadruple-choke Weber carburettors with their gauze-covered intake trumpets, one for each cylinder below.

The 250MM was also produced in spider form by Vignale and chassis number 0274MM is seen in these two pictures. It was completely different in approach to the Pinin Farina version and virtually indistinguishable from the 166MM and 340MM Vignale spiders. This particular example has twin portholes on the wing sides, whereas three were more common, and also a cut-away rear bulkhead to enable the driver's seat to be moved further back. In the May 1954 issue of *Road & Track* magazine a 0–60mph time of 5.1 secs was recorded for a 250MM Vignale spider, with the comment from the Technical Editor, 'Never before have I accelerated so rapidly, travelled so fast, or decelerated so suddenly.'

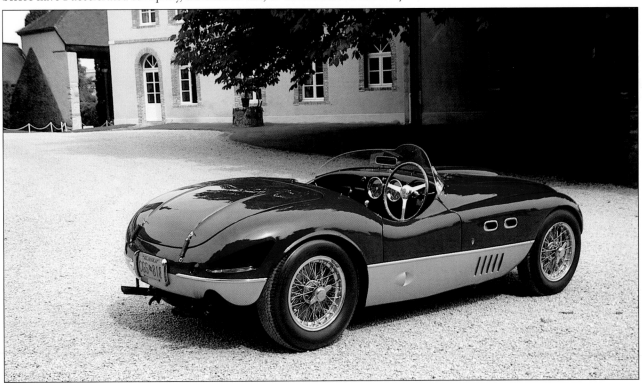

This is a 340MM Vignale spider, chassis number 0280AM, carrying the race number with which it won the 1953 Mille Miglia in the hands of Marzotto/Crosara. Once again the resemblance to the 166MM and 250MM is evident but it is worth comparing the pictures to note the detail differences that occurred on this style of body.

This is yet another variation on the Vignale spider theme, a 625TF, chassis number 0304TF, of which only two spiders were built in 1953, and this is the only known survivor. This used a four-cylinder 2.5-litre capacity engine, hence the 625 single cylinder cubic capacity model designation. Vignale also built a coupé version of this model which resembled the spider with a higher windscreen and fastback roof running into the tail panel. This model marked the first time that Ferrari had used a four-cylinder engine in a sports or GT car, although they had plenty of experience in Formula 1 single seaters.

The 735S was the next four-cylinder Ferrari sports racing car, three examples of which were produced in 1953. This is chassis number 0444MD with a Pinin Farina spider body. The model number 735 refers to the cubic capacity of one cylinder, hence the total capacity of the engine is 2.94 litres.

The 1953–4 Pinin Farina-designed 375MM berlinetta was produced with a number of minor detail differences to the bodies of individual cars, but the overall shape remained true to the original concept. Chassis number 0358AM is seen here. The headlights of 375 models were normally under Plexiglas covers, whereas those of the 250MMs were normally uncovered and the two models had different rear wing profiles, but there are exceptions. The engine was basically that of the 340 model, increased in capacity by lengthening the stroke to produce a 4.5-litre unit.

The Hawthorn/Maglioli 375MM Pinin Farina berlinetta, chassis number 0320AM, on its way to win the 1953 Pescara 12 Hour Race. The headlights on this car are an exception to the standard headlight treatment, with the units further recessed into the wings under larger Plexiglas covers.

This 375MM Pinin Farina berlinetta, chassis number 0378AM, was built in 1954. It has been 'civilized' for road use with the addition of front and rear bumpers and also the radiator grille shape has been altered and the carburettor air intake on the bonnet is of a different profile.

The 375MM was also produced by Pinin Farina as a spider, which had a similar frontal aspect to their berlinetta version with an aggressive grille and headlights in the wing extremities under Plexiglas covers. Chassis number 0370AM is seen here. The twin rows of rivets running from the grille to the corners of the bonnet aperture increase its sense of purpose. The hinged flap just forward of the bonnet is for access to the radiator cap.

The rear view of 375MM Pinin Farina spider, chassis number 0376AM, in the colourful livery in which it competed in the last Carrera Panamericana road race in 1954, when it was driven by Luigi Chinetti with John Shakespeare to fourth place overall. The race was won by Umberto Maglioli in a similar car. In 1954 an upgraded version of this model was introduced which had a 4.9-litre engine coupled to a four-speed transaxle, with a different Pinin Farina-designed spider body, and was called the 375 Plus, an example of which won the Le Mans Race in the same year.

The engine bay of the 375MM is dominated by the beautifully crafted aluminium air-cleaner box astride the triple Weber four-choke carburettors in the centre of the vee formed by the cylinder heads with the angled magnettos driven off the end of the camshafts, visible at the rear of the engine.

A selection of Ferrari sales brochures produced during the early years of the company.

Chapter 2

THE PININFARINA
INFLUENCE

The 250 Europa model with Pinin Farina bodywork was presented at the 1953 Paris Salon. A single Pinin Farina cabriolet was also made and three Vignale-bodied coupés in late 1953 and through 1954. This model used a 3-litre V12 engine developed from the Lampredi long block engine design. This was the first model to incorporate a degree of standardization in the body style, which is also apparent in the concurrently produced 375 America model and marks the start of the major Pinin Farina influence on Ferrari bodywork.

Introduction

By 1954 the majority of roadgoing Ferraris were bodied to the designs of Pinin Farina, with Scaglietti handling the sports racing models. From then until 1973, when the Bertone-designed 308GT4 was announced, the design efforts of other houses were rarely used and when they were it was normally only on a one-off basis for a specific car, perhaps at the behest of a particularly valued client.

The reasons for this commitment to essentially one design house was probably the result of a number of factors. In 1953 production exceeded fifty cars in a year for the first time and some form of rationalization was necessary to give the marque an identity as opposed to the name of the designer taking precedence. Pinin Farina had the facilities and experience necessary for a more streamlined production-line philosophy, rather than the artisinal approach of very small-scale production spread between a number of suppliers. In theory the rationalization would produce a higher quality, more coherent product, with a distinct Ferrari identity continued with more constant costings.

The first fruits of this philosophy were the 250 Europa and 375 America models, which carried essentially the same body on a common chassis, only the engine size being different. These were announced at the 1953 Paris Salon, with production continuing into late 1954. Vignale also bodied three examples of each model, as well as a single 375 America cabriolet, but these virtually signalled the end of their relationship with Ferrari, apart from a 250 Europa GT for the Belgian Princess Liliane De Rethy in 1954 and a shooting-brake based on a 330GT 2+2 in 1968.

The 250 Europa developed into the 250 Europa GT, announced at the 1954 Paris Salon, which was visually very similar but on a 2,600 mm wheelbase, as opposed to the 2,800 mm of its predecessor. The reduction in wheelbase was made possible by the deletion of the 375 America model from the range and the use of a newly developed, short block, type 112, 3-litre V12 engine, based on the original Colombo design. It may be recalled that the original Colombo design had push-fit cylinder liners, whereas the Lampredi engines had the cylinder liners screwed into the cylinder heads, which took up more space, necessitating a greater block length. The development of this engine in the 250 series of models was to form the backbone of Ferrari production for the next decade. During this period it was seen in numerous guises, with sparkplugs inside and outside the vee, wet and dry sumps, and three or six twin-choke carburettors, to name but a few, each variation having a specific engine type reference number.

The 250 Europa GT also had competition berlinetta derivatives produced consecutively that initially bore the mark of the 250MM berlinetta. This developed into a style that would carry through into the next series of competition berlinettas and became known as the 'Tour de France' models owing to their successive victories in the gruelling event in the late 1950s. In 1956 the 250 Europa GT coupés were replaced with the 250GT coupé, also by Pinin Farina, although only a few early examples were constructed by them as their premises were undergoing redevelopment, and the production was put in the hands of first Carrozzeria Boano and then Carrozzeria

Ellena. The bodies are all very similar with the Boanos being known as 'low roof' and the Ellenas as 'high roof' because of the increased cabin height on the latter model. A two-seater 250GT cabriolet was produced by Pinin Farina concurrently with these models and at the end of 1957 a second open 250GT model joined the range. This was called the 250GT California spider, based on the competition Tour de France berlinetta underpinnings and, although based on a Pinin Farina design, was modified by and the model constructed by Scaglietti, together with the competition cars. In 1957 another milestone was reached in production terms as for the first time more than a hundred cars were produced (the actual figure was 113) in a year.

In 1958 Pinin Farina became Pininfarina and introduced a new 250GT coupé, very similar in appearance to the second series 250GT cabriolet that followed it in 1959, whereas visually the preceding coupés and cabriolets had shared no common elements. Although the 250GT series, in coupé, cabriolet, Tour de France berlinetta and California spider forms, made up the bulk of production, there were still more exclusive larger engined models produced in limited quantities, and Bertone, Ghia and Zagato still managed to style the occasional car. The larger engined models were the 410 Superamerica, with a 5-litre V12 engine that carried a variety of body styles in the second half of the 1950s. Some were true one-offs, such as the very Americanized example from Ghia in 1956 on chassis number 0473SA with its enormous tail fins, the Pinin Farina 410 Superfast, chassis number 0483SA, of the same year and similarly attired, while Scaglietti offered a variation on the fins theme in 1957 on the 410 Superamerica chassis number 0671SA. The bulk of the Superamerica production, if just over thirty cars in four years can be called bulk, carried more conservative Pinin Farina-designed coachwork with a family resemblance to the 250GT range, although the price was about 50 per cent more. Carrozzeria Boano also tried their hand on the 410SA, to produce one coupé and one cabriolet carrying very similar bodies. These large engined, top end of the market cars were aimed at finding favour with the American clientele, a lucrative sales ground. This market had been explored in the formative years of the company by Luigi Chinetti, a man responsible for swelling the Ferrari coffers with thousands of dollars over a number of years, and reputedly the instigator of production of Ferrari cars for sale to finance the racing operation.

By the end of the decade production had risen to nearly 250 cars a year, the number of staff increasing from 250 in 1955 to over 350, and the pen of Pinin Farina was, virtually without exception, the only one that created Ferrari road-car body styles.

The 375 America that was introduced with the 250 Europa was identical in appearance. Both cars had a 2,800 mm wheelbase chassis, which was the longest ever built by Ferrari up to that time, and really only necessary for the 375 version because of the length of its 4.5-litre engine. However, to try and standardize production it was used for both models. Vignale also bodied three coupés and one cabriolet, while Ghia tried their hand on one coupé.

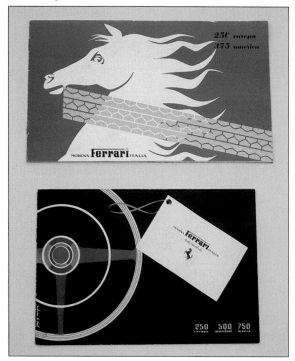

Factory sales brochures. The upper one is for the 250 Europa and 375 America, while the lower one promotes the succeeeding 250 Europa GT together with its competition stablemates the 500 Mondial and 750 Monza.

The next evolution in the 250 series was the 250 Europa GT which is very similar in overall appearance to the preceding 250 Europa model and was introduced at the Paris Salon in 1954. It was produced through to the beginning of 1956. The new model used a 3-litre V12 engine derived from the original Colombo short block design. With the deletion of the 375 America from the range and this shorter engine they were able to reduce the wheelbase of the chassis by 200 mm to 2,600 mm which also had the benefit of improving the handling. Originally this model had transverse leaf-spring front suspension but this was changed to coil springs during the production run. Apart from a single Vignale coupé for the Belgian Princess Liliane de Rethy, on chassis number 0359GT, all other models in the series were designed by Pinin Farina.

Another example of a 250 Europa GT berlinetta, on chassis number 0393GT, which is even closer in concept to the next series of competition berlinettas. This car was displayed at the 1955 Paris Salon and was built for the head of the Dubonnet drinks concern. Even though there is plenty of chrome, its use doesn't overpower the lines of the car but accentuates certain features.

Pinin Farina also produced variations on the 250 Europa GT theme with seven aluminium-bodied competition berlinettas. They had varying body configurations, often with much of their 250MM berlinetta in the overall shape, and are usually regarded as design studies for the 1956 Tour de France berlinettas. The similarities with the 250MM berlinetta can be seen in the example seen here, chassis number 0415GT.

In 1954 Ghia produced this unique coupé on a 375MM, chassis number 0476AM. Although on an even number competition chassis, this bulky body was obviously not intended for competition, a further example of the cross pollination between road and competition cars of the period. This salmon pink and grey creation was displayed on the Ghia stand at the 1955 Turin Salon.

This is a unique Pinin Farina-bodied 375MM, chassis number 0456AM, painted a special oyster gold colour and ordered by the Italian film director Roberto Rossellini for the actress Ingrid Bergman in 1954, although she never took delivery. As can be seen from the even chassis number, this car was constructed on a competition chassis, although from its appearance it is obviously a very stylish road car. This reinforces the theory that the divide between road and competition cars of the period was very narrow. It is widely thought that this was a landmark design for Pinin Farina and incorporated styling elements that would be found in various Ferrari road cars for years afterwards, including retractable headlights and the sweeping buttresses from the roof into the rear wing line.

The 250 Monza was an amalgam of the chassis from the four-cylinder 750 Monza and the 3-litre V12 250 engine. Two examples were built in 1954 with competition spider bodywork by Scaglietti. When compared to the similar Scaglietti bodies for the Mondial and Monzas, it can be seen that the radiator grille is deeper and that there is a raised section in the bonnet over the carburettors. This example is chassis number 0466M.

Pinin Farina bodied a further two 250 Monzas in a style identical to the one that they used for their interpretation of the 500 Mondial, apart from an air intake on the bonnet. This in turn was a scaled-down version of the body used on the 375MM. Chassis number 0420MD is seen here.

The 500 Mondial version of this Pinin Farina body design, on chassis number 0434MD, can be identified by the large bore exhaust system on the left side of the car. These were the final interpretations by Pinin Farina on an open two-seater sports racing Ferrari and for the remainder of the 1950s these models were designed and built by Scaglietti, who became the official competition body shop of Ferrari. Most of the competition berlinettas designed by Pinin Farina were also built by Scaglietti.

A 750 Monza, chassis number 0520M, which is visually virtually identical to the 500 Mondial. The major difference between the two models was the size of the four-cylinder engine, which, with a 750 model reference, was of 3-litre capacity. The Monza version of the engine had a wider angle between the inlet and exhaust camshafts but this would not be discernible to the average viewer. A comment equally applicable to both models is that the small wrap-around screen was sometimes replaced by a full-width screen, particularly if the car was raced after 1956, when the sport's governing body decreed a full-width screen mandatory.

The best-known configuration of the 500 Mondial with the Scaglietti spider body is seen here on chassis number 0468MD. These cars were powered by a Lampredi-designed four-cylinder engine of 2-litre capacity, again the model number referred to the capacity of a single cylinder. The engine had twin overhead camshafts with a wide angle between the cam covers, twin

spark plugs per cylinder, a pair of Weber twin-choke side draught carburettors on the right side and a large bore tubular exhaust manifold on the left which fed into the main pipe visible beneath the car.

An 857 Monza from 1955 with a 3.43-litre engine, on chassis number 0578M. The Scaglietti-built body is far more bulbous than the 750 version, with a much deeper radiator grille flanked by brake cooling duct openings. The 860 Monzas of 1956 are very similar in appearance, in fact almost identical. This is chassis number 0578M.

At a glance very similar to the 500 Mondial/750 Monza, this 121LM is a six-cylinder variant on the theme and is seen here at Le Mans in 1955, where they all retired. These straight six-engined machines had a very short and relatively undistinguished racing career in 1955. They had a wheelbase 150 mm longer than the Mondial/Monza at 2,400 mm to accommodate the longer engine and a five-speed transaxle instead of the four-speed unit of the four-cylinder cars. Initially the engine capacity was 3.75 litres and the model was referred to as the 118LM, but within a very short space of time a new 4.4-litre unit had been built and the title changed to 121LM.

At the end of 1955 the 121LMs were rebodied by Scaglietti and sold to private clients. This example, chassis number 0484LM, was sold to American enthusiast Tony Parravano and is seen here in his team livery. The rebodying of this car can be seen to include a reshaped radiator grille and the addition of a fin to the headrest cowl.

The 410S spider produced in 1956 had a 4.96-litre V12 engine coupled to a five-speed transaxle. Two examples were built but were only raced once by the factory in Buenos Aires before being sold to private clients.

The 1956 sports racing 500 Testa Rossa with a Scaglietti aluminium body and 2-litre four-cylinder engine. The model name 500 Testa Rossa combined the cubic capacity of one cylinder, 500cc, with Testa Rossa ('red head'), a reference to the colour that the cam covers were painted. As with the preceding four-cylinder Mondial/Monzas the engine was a twin overhead camshaft unit, fitted with a pair of sidedraught twin-choke carburettors, but had coil ignition instead of magnettos, and the gearbox was mounted to the engine with a rigid rear axle. This was the first model in the Testa Rossa series.

In 1957 the 500TR had changes made to the bodywork to meet the sport's governing body's new appendix 'C' regulations. The model designation became 500TRC, the C referring to the model's compliance with the new regulations. Visually it is hardly different to its predecessor, the main identifying feature being the flat bonnet line of the 500TRC compared with the twin bulges of the 500TR. The shape of the radiator opening is also slightly different and the 500TRC has more pronounced curves to the front wing line.

For the Le Mans Race in 1956 regulations permitted the use of 2.5-litre engines, thus Ferrari built three 500TRs fitted with 2.5-litre four-cylinder engines, which are referred to by some as 625TRs and by others as 625LMs. The engine used was the unit from the type 625 Formula 1 car, while bodily the Scaglietti version is identical to the 500TR.

This 625TR/LM, chassis number 0642MDTR, carries a Touring spider body which differs from the Scaglietti version mainly in the shape of the nose, the scalloped front wings behind the wheels and the lower trailing edge to the tail.

Although the four-cylinder sports racing models were the spearhead of the Ferrari campaign between 1954 and '57, as can be seen V12-engined sports racing models were also being produced. In 1957 there were the visually similar 315S and 335S models. Once again the number in the model reference relates to the cubic capacity of a single cylinder, hence the 315S had a 3.78-litre unit and the 335S a 4.02-litre unit. This example is a 335S, chassis number 0700, with spider bodywork by Scaglietti. A 315S won the last Mille Miglia in 1957 and was driven by Piero Taruffi. In 1958 some examples were fitted with pontoon-fender bodywork to resemble the new 250 Testa Rossa model of that year.

The 290MM was originally produced in 1956, with a 3.5-litre V12 engine and a Scaglietti spider body very similar to the 500TRs, but, as with the 315S and 335S, a rebody in the style of the 1958 250 Testa Rossa wasn't out of the question. The 1956 Mille Miglia was won by Eugenio Castelotti in a 290MM. Seen here is chassis number 0628, still wearing its 1958 Testa Rossa-style rebody.

The 1958 pontoon-fendered 250 Testa Rossa with Scaglietti spider body and a 3-litre V12 engine based on the original Colombo design, which would eventually develop into the motive power for the widely aclaimed 250GTO berlinetta in 1962. Sergio Scaglietti regards this body as one of his most pleasing efforts. A 250 Testa Rossa won the 1958 Le Mans 24 Hour Race driven by Phil Hill/Olivier Gendebien, albeit with a different nose treatment as the pontoon wings were found to induce front end instability at high speed – beautiful sculptures in metal, but aerodynamically unsound. This is chassis number 0718TR.

The 1959 version of the 250 Testa Rossa carried a Fantuzzi-built body that was a development of the revised nose treatment of the 1958 model. Now the row of carburettor intake trumpets are clearly visible through the clear Plexiglas bonnet intake. Under the skin the new model had a five-speed gearbox coupled to the engine with De Dion rear suspension, replacing the former model's four-speed transaxle. The factory developed some of these models into interim versions for the 1960 car, which are known as 250TR 59/60s. This is chassis number 0770TR.

Almost identical to the 250TR and produced concurrently were the 196S and 246S Dino sports racing models. With these models the model number has a different meaning. For the Dino the first two figures are the total engine capacity in litres and the last figure the number of cylinders, hence the 246S is a 2.4-litre V6 engine (all Dino models had vee configuration engines), the S in the name referring to Sport. The easiest way to tell the difference between a Dino and a 250TR with similar bodywork is to count the number of intake trumpets under the Plexiglas cover on the bonnet: the Dino had six and the 250 Testa Rossa had twelve. American driver Richie Ginther is seen here, in chassis number 0784, during the 1960 Nurburgring 1,000km race.

While the 250GT series formed the mainstream production coupé road cars and competition berlinettas during the latter half of the 1950s, there was still a series of low-production volume, large-engined coupés produced which developed from the 375 America models. These were called the 410SA models, with a 4.9-litre V12 engine, and although most were bodied by Pinin Farina this is one of the exceptions on chassis number 0473SA, which received this very American-influenced wildly finned body by Ghia. Scaglietti also produced a one-off 410SA in 1957, on chassis number 0671SA, which was more subdued than the Ghia offering, but still sported high fins on the rear wings.

Pinin Farina showed that they could play with fins when they presented this white over metallic blue exercise called the 410SA Superfast, built on chassis number 0483SA, at the 1956 Paris Salon. Note that there are no windscreen pillars, only the screen frame and the roof is cantilevered from the rear section as on the 212 'Uovo' produced by Reggiani in 1950.

The less radical 410SA production cars from Pinin Farina had a body style very similar to their 250GT cousins, the main differentiating features being the rear window shape, the intake on the bonnet and the large fancy exhaust vents on the front wing sides. However, examples of the 250GT sometimes incorporate one or the other of these latter two features. This model was produced on both 2,800 mm and 2,600 mm wheelbase chassis, known as series I and series II models. Clients for this exclusive model included the Shah of Persia.

The 1957 interpretation on the 410SA by Pinin Farina was much more rounded in profile as can be seen from chassis number 0719SA, being exhibited at the Paris and Turin salons. A very similar body graced a 250GT specially built for Prince Bernhard of the Netherlands on chassis number 0725GT, although his car was painted black. In both cases they were built on a 2,600 mm wheelbase chassis.

Carrozzeria Boano created a pair of almost identical 410SA bodies in 1956, one a cabriolet on chassis number 0485SA as seen here, and the other a coupé on chassis number 0477SA. Once again rear wing fins featured but they weren't as extreme as their contemporaries. The small diameter headlights look rather lost on the large plain front bodywork.

The final evolution in the 410SA run was the Series III model, introduced at the 1958 Paris Salon. Pininfarina had redesigned the bodywork with a lower and wider radiator grille, the rear wing profile was changed and the wrap-around rear screen disappeared. All these cars have individual differences and were available with either open headlights or Plexiglas covered units.

In 1956 the Pinin Farina factory was undergoing redevelopment and they didn't have the production capacity for their newly designed Ferrari 250GT coupé. The production was passed over to Carrozzeria Boano and hence the model became known as the 250GT Boano coupé, being produced by them into 1957, before Mario Boano handed the business over to his son-in-law Ezio Ellena. With the change in company name the model also received some styling changes and became known as the 250GT Ellena. The crossover from road car to competition can be seen in this picture of Camillo Luglio competing in the 1956 Mille Miglia in his 250GT Boano.

53

The 250GT Boano has become known as the 'low-roof' model and the 250GT Ellena the 'high-roof' model. This rear view of a 250GT Boano emphasizes the low roof line and also clearly shows the other easy identification feature, the quarter lights in the door glass. The exhaust vents on the wing sides are not common to all cars.

The 250GT Ellena is virtually identical to the 250GT Boano but the deeper windscreen owing to the raised roof line should be noted, although the lack of a quarter light in the door glass is the most obvious identifiable feature. Production ceased in 1958 to make way for a new 250GT coupé that would be built by Pininfarina, their new plant having been completed and begun production.

During the latter part of the 1950s Pinin farina produced quite an array of one-off bodies on the 250GT chassis. This example, built on chassis number 0751GT, for Princess Liliane de Rethy of Belgium, is very similar to the 410SA, chassis number 0719SA, except for the rear wing line and tail treatment.

The first of the 1956 Pinin Farina-designed, Scaglietti-built, 250GT competition berlinettas on the 2,600 mm wheelbase chassis. It is very similar in appearance to the 250 Europa GT berlinettas, with strong traces of the 250/340/375MM examples as shown here on chassis number 0557GT. This was the start of a line of 250GT berlinettas that would dominate the 3-litre GT category until 1964. In 1956 one of these berlinettas won the Tour de France Auto. After a victory the organizers gave the manufacturer the right to use the name 'Tour de France' in the model title if they wished, hence this series of models became known as the 250GT Tour de France berlinettas.

The early 1957 version of the 250GT TdF competition berlinetta retained a front very similar to the 1956 model. However, the rear was completely restyled with a smaller rear screen, fourteen louvres on the sail panels and reprofiled rear wings incorporating vertical tail lights. This is the second of the new series of cars, chassis number 0597GT.

This is an example of the development from the original TdF competition 250GT berlinetta, seen here at the Nurburgring in 1957 driven by Michel Ringoir. It still has the low headlight position in the wing extremity but the rear wing line has altered, the wrap-around rear screen has gone and the sail panel has fourteen exhaust air louvres.

In mid-1957 the 250GT Tour de France berlinetta received a revised front wing line, with the headlights raised to the top wing edge and recessed under Plexiglas covers. Concurrently the louvre arrangement on the sail panel changed to a three-outlet layout and the boot profile changed with the fuel filler becoming exposed in the top left corner of the lid, as seen here on chassis number 0763GT.

Between 1956 and '59 Zagato bodied a total of five 250GT Tour de France berlinettas, each body being different. This example, with the traditional Zagato 'double-bubble' roofline, was built in 1956 on chassis number 0537GT.

In the spring of 1958 the 250GT Tour de France berlinetta had the sail-panel exhaust-louvre arrangement changed again to a single unit, as seen here on chassis number 1035GT, complete with appropriate numberplate. Cold-air

induction, via the bonnet scoop, was a feature of all but the earliest of these models.

This is a fine example of an early 1958 three-louvre 250GT Tour de France berlinetta, chassis number 0879GT, fitted with bumpers which the majority don't carry. Apart from the five cars produced by Zagato, all the others in the Tour de France series were manufactured by Scaglietti in aluminium to a Pinin Farina design, and all had left-hand drive.

Many historic competition Ferraris still get regular historic-race exercise and the 250GT TdF competition berlinetta is no exception. This is chassis number 1385GT at Spa-Francorchamps.

For 1959 there were two distinct versions of the 250GT berlinetta, the first being virtually identical to the 1958 model, except that due to a change in Italian lighting legislation, the headlights were uncovered at the wing extremities, although foreign customers could still specify covered lights. Some earlier cars were changed to an open-light layout during this period. The second model is what has come to be referred to as the 'Interim' model. Only seven of these cars were produced during 1959, with a completely different berlinetta body designed by Pininfarina. This body evolved into that of the 250GT SWB model for the 1960 model year. Below is an 'Interim' chassis number 1509GT and the most obvious difference to its successor is recognizable – the rear quarter light in the sail panel to the rear of the door glass.

Alongside the mainly steel-bodied road coupés and aluminium competition berlinettas there was a range of 250GT cabriolets related to the road coupés and California spiders related to the competition berlinettas. The series 1 cabriolets had bodies similar in style to the one-off coupé produced for the Princess Liliane de Rethy, while the series 2 cabriolets had a style almost identical to its coupé counterpart that replaced the 250GT Ellena coupé in 1958. The 250GT California was built on the same 2,600 mm wheelbase chassis as the competition berlinettas and were replaced by a visually very similar model on the succeeding 2,400 mm wheelbase chassis in 1960. Either model was available with the option of open or covered headlights. The example seen here is a 250GT California spider on a 2,600 mm wheelbase, chassis number 1459GT.

The 250GT Pininfarina coupé that replaced the 250GT Ellena model in 1958 was the first Ferrari body to be produced at their new Grugliasco plant on the outskirts of Turin. The most notable feature was a lowering of the waist line, which provided an airy cockpit with slim screen pillars, and, although built on a chassis of the same wheelbase, the new model was 50 mm shorter than its predecessor. The cabriolet version was virtually identical, albeit with a folding roof. Some examples of both models featured a shallow bonnet scoop. Production of the coupé continued into 1960, while the cabriolet stayed in production until 1962. *Road & Track* magazine road tested this model in June 1960 and recorded a 0–60mph time of 7.1 seconds, with a top speed of 126mph.

Chapter 3

THROUGH THE 1960S – 250GT SWB TO 365GT 2+2

The Pininfarina-designed, Scaglietti-built, 250GT berlinetta, announced at the 1959 Paris Salon for the 1960 model year, was built on a new 2,400 mm wheelbase chassis and has since become known as the 250GT SWB berlinetta. The SWB stands for 'short wheelbase' and the term LWB for 'long wheelbase' – these descriptions are applied to the 1956–9 berlinettas to differentiate between them. The shape of the new berlinetta had been seen in the last of the old models but it had lost the quarter light behind the door glass with the reduction in wheelbase. The early cars in the series had no exhaust outlets on the wing sides or brake cooling ducts in the front apron, but many have since been modified to incorporate either or both of these features. For 1961 quarter lights were provided in the door glass and the trailing upper edge of the door window was given a smoother line. A 1961 competition berlinetta, chassis number 2869GT, is seen here at the 1962 Le Mans test day, where it was driven by Jean Guichet and Pierre Noblet.

Introduction

At his annual end of season press conference in 1959 Enzo Ferrari presented a new small capacity, four-cylinder engine, with the logo 854 on the camshaft cover, 85 for the cubic capacity of 850cc and 4 for the number of cylinders. This was proposed to be the powerplant for a new small Ferrari for the masses, although there was no intention that the car would be manufactured by Ferrari. By the middle of 1960 the engine had been grafted into a modified Fiat chassis (shades of the 1940 Auto Avio Costruzione 815) and Pininfarina had clothed the combination in an elegant coupé body, the resultant baby Ferrari being dubbed the 'Ferrarina'. The next development of this project was the display of a Bertone-designed coupé at the Turin Salon in October 1961, by which time the engine capacity had been increased to 973cc and was known as the Mille. The car stirred interest in Dr de Nora, a long-standing client of Ferrari, who bought the project and formed Autocostruzione Societa per Azioni, better known as ASA. Production of the ASA 1000GT started in a factory in Milan, headed by the founder's son, but production never really took off and the company collapsed in 1967, by which time only about 140 cars had been produced.

Things were brighter in Maranello as the 250GT SWB berlinetta, announced at the 1959 Paris Salon, started proving its worth on the racetracks in 1960. It carried on the winning ways of its predecessor, leading to a healthy demand for the competition and road versions. In 1960 the 250GT coupé was deleted from the range, although the cabriolet continued in production until 1962. With the demise of the 250GT coupé, a new 2+2 coupé was introduced, the 250GTE, of which nearly 1,000 were manufactured before production ceased in 1963. The final fifty examples of this model were fitted with the 4-litre engine of the upcoming 330GT 2+2 and were called the 330 America 2+2, although externally there was no visible difference to the 3-litre version. At the 1962 Paris Salon a new two-seater berlinetta was introduced to replace the street version of the 250GT SWB, as the competition version had already been succeeded by the 250GTO. This was the 250GT/L berlinetta, the 'L' standing for *lusso* ('luxury'), and subsequently this model has generally been referred to as the 250GT Lusso, which was helped to distinguish it from its predecessor. Production started in early 1963 and ran through until 1964. The body style of this model, with an altered nose profile similar to that of the 250GTO, was also used to clothe one 250GTO and four 330LM competition berlinettas.

In 1962 production figures almost reached 500 cars, with a stated output of 493 cars. The next year saw the 500 unit barrier broken with an output of 598 cars, while the remainder of the decade saw fluctuations of up to a hundred cars a year, but the annual figure never dropped below the 600 mark.

The arrival of the 1960s also saw a virtually complete road-car design monopoly by Pininfarina, the only exceptions during the decade being a one-off Bertone design of a 250GT SWB berlinetta, chassis number 3269GT, in 1961, which followed their 1960 one-off 250GT SW berlinetta on chassis number 1739GT, Zagato's 'Spider Speciale', and Vignale's one-off station wagon, based on a 330GT 2+2 coupé, chassis number 07963, in 1968. The final development of the 250GT competition coupé, the

250GTO, was based on a design by Giotto Bizzarrini and then developed into its production form by Scaglietti after Bizzarrini, Chiti and others were dismissed by Enzo Ferrari in November 1961. In late 1963 Pininfarina redesigned the bodywork for the 250GTO, to produce what is normally referred to as the 1964 body, very similar in appearance to the mid-engined 250LM that was introduced at about the same time.

Production of the small series large-engined and luxurious GT cars continued alongside the 250GT series, with the 400 Superfast between 1960 and '62, as well as a unique 400 Superamerica spider, chassis number 2311SA, almost identical to a 250GT California spider, for Ferrari director Michel Paul-Cavallier in 1960. These were complemented, and succeeded, by the 400 Superamerica Aerodinamico series 1 and 2 coupés and cabriolets, produced until 1964. The final phase of these leviathans of the road came with the 500 Superfast coupé produced between 1964 and '66 and the swansong 365 California spider between 1966 and '67. From 1967 until 1984, when the limited production 288GTO was introduced, Ferrari didn't produce any special models outside the normal range, unless they were show cars, competition development cars, or prototypes.

The 250GT series came to an end in 1964 and was replaced by the two-seater 275GTB berlinetta and 275GTS spider and the 2+2 330GT coupé. The 275GTB spawned a competition derivative, the 275GTB/C, and received a four camshaft engine in 1966, becoming the 275GTB/4 and, upon the instigation of Luigi Chinetti, a spider version of this was produced called the 275GTB/4 NART spider. In 1966 two new models joined the range, the 330GTC coupé and the 330GTS spider, which in late 1968 became the 365GTC and 365GTS, with the adoption of larger engines and minor body changes. On the 2+2 front, the 330GT 2+2 was replaced by the 365GT 2+2 in 1967. At the 1968 Paris Salon the top of the range 365GTB/4 Daytona was announced, which would be the last large capacity front-engined, two-seater Ferrari for nearly three decades.

An important development took place in the mid-1960s when Pininfarina displayed a small mid-engined coupé at the 1965 Paris Salon carrying the badge Dino, in memory of Dino Ferrari, the badge script being a stylized version of his signature. This would develop through a series of prototypes with longitudinal engine placements to the definitive production Dino 206GT, with a transverse mid-engine configuration, in 1968. This layout was to form the backbone of major series V6 and V8 Ferrari production for two decades until the 348 and Mondial t models were announced with longitudinal mid-engines.

Between 1960 and '68 production had more than doubled and the limited series cars had gradually been phased out. However, the broadly spread racing programme consumed much of the profits and Ferrari needed an infusion of capital and a rationalization of its racing activities to carry it into the 1970s.

This rear view of the second right-hand drive 250GT SWB-built, chassis number 1995GT, shows clearly the difference in the curve of the top trailing edge of the door window frame on an early car. The 250GT SWB berlinetta was built in both aluminium competition and steel-bodied street versions, although some street cars had a number of aluminium panels if requested by the client. Similarly, the client could also request differences in the state of tune of the engine and rear axle

ratio, making for quite a diverse range of possible specifications on this model. The steel-bodied street version was effectively a replacement for the 250GT coupé. Apart from the standard-bodied Pininfarina-designed berlinettas, there were also two different Bertone examples and Pininfarina also produced variants with 400SA coupé Aerodinamica-style bodywork.

The engine bay of a 250GT SWB competition model. It is dominated by the gleaming aluminium cold-air box into which the bonnet intake feeds air to the triple twin-choke carburettors, with gauze-covered intake trumpets; some later competition models were fitted with a six twin-choke carburettor layout. The raised Ferrari script in polished aluminium is cast into the black crackle-finish cam covers.

This is a one-off 250GT cabriolet produced by Pininfarina on an SWB chassis number 1737GT in 1960, with bodywork similar to the 400SA cabriolet produced between 1959 and '61. A very elegant slim-pillared removable hardtop, featuring a glazed panel in the roof, was also provided.

A further derivation of the cabriolet theme on a 250GT SWB chassis was this 'Spider Speciale' from Zagato on chassis number 2491GT, a radical design, but hardly beautiful.

This is Pininfarina's 250GT berlinetta 'Speciale Le Mans', which is very similar to their 400SA design and was built on a 250GT SWB chassis number 2643GT for the 1961 Le Mans Race. It is generally regarded as an early design study for the 1962 250GTO.

When Count Volpi was told by Enzo Ferrari that he wasn't going to allow him to have the 250GTO that he had on order for his team to race in the 1962 GT Manufacturers' Championship, he employed Ing. Giotto Bizzarrini to develop his 250GT SWB chassis number 2819GT. This was the result of his efforts – by lowering the engine-mounting height and moving it further back in the frame he achieved a very low frontal area, while the virtually straight roofline running into an abrupt Kamm tail earned it the nickname 'bread van'.

Sometimes when a 250GT SWB was crashed while racing the owner would employ a coachbuilder to replace the standard body with a more slippery one in the hope that it would prove faster than before. Piero Drogo in Modena was one such bodyshop that rebodied damaged 250GT SWBs with his own concoctions. This Drogo body was fitted to chassis number 2735GT, the second Stirling Moss/Rob Walker 250GT SWB, when owned by Chris Kerrison, who is seen here driving it at Brands Hatch in 1963.

The 250GT SWB California spider is seen here in open headlight form on chassis number 2505GT. This example has a split front bumper but a single-piece unit was more standard wear and sometimes rubber-faced overriders were provided. The carburettor air-intake slot on the bonnet was a feature of all models, whether long or short wheelbase.

The 250GTO is one of the best-known Ferraris ever produced, the tight sensual curves, when coupled with the numerous sculpted intakes and slots, exude an air of great purpose. This is chassis number 3527GT with appropriate British registration plate.

The 250GTO is beautiful from any angle, with its full curves, carefully sculpted slots, minimal decoration and elegant spoiler above the lightly recessed Kamm tail, giving it a tremendous presence and sense of purpose. The body design was the work of Scaglietti, based on a concept developed by Ing. Giotto Bizzarrini when he worked in the factory racing department. This is chassis number 5111GT, bearing an appropriate New York registration number.

The legendary 250GTO of 1962, on chassis number 3589GT, being driven by Mike Parkes to victory in the Peco Trophy Race at Brands Hatch in August 1962. Thirty-six 3-litre engined cars were produced, as well as three 4-litre engined examples, between 1962 and '64. The GTO was the ultimate expression of the 250GT competition berlinetta, winning the Manufacturers' Championship for Ferrari in 1962, '63 and '64. This model achieved a record of another kind in 1989, by setting a world record for the highest price ever paid for a car, when one was sold for ten million pounds.

This is a 1964 rebody on chassis number 4399GT, the first car to be modified in this way. This example features cold-air induction to the carburettors via the bonnet intake, a short roof with inbuilt spoiler and is finished in the colours of the British importer's, Maranello Concessionaires Ltd, racing team – red with a Cambridge blue stripe.

For the 1964 season four 1962-bodied 250GTOs were rebodied and a further three new cars constructed with a new body style designed by Pininfarina and constructed by Scaglietti. The new body was wider and lower than the 1962 version and featured a wider track but didn't show any appreciable difference in performance. The design is very similar to that used for the mid-engined 250LM model. Two of the rebodied cars featured a long roof, with a deeply tunnelled rear screen, one of which is seen here on chassis number 4675GT during the 1964 Targa Florio. The other examples featured slight differences in body details, mainly relative to the bonnet blister and short-roof profile. This model was the end of the 250GT front-engined competition car series.

The 330LM berlinetta designed by Pininfarina in 1963 had a 4-litre V12 engine and the body style was an amalgam of the style of the 250GT Lusso from the cabin rearward, with a nose section very similar to a 250GTO. Four examples were produced and this body style also clothed one 250GTO. Initially they were built without a tail spoiler but after tests one was added to three of the cars that were raced, to improve high-speed stability. The fourth car was only used as a road car and never received the spoiler, nor did it have the supplementary driving lights under Plexiglas covers in the nose. During the Le Mans test day in 1963 a 330LM berlinetta, driven by Mike Parkes, was the first car to break the 300kph barrier on the Mulsanne Straight. The picture below shows Lorenzo Bandini in the only right-hand drive example produced, chassis number 4725SA, at Brands Hatch in August 1963.

The 250LM berlinetta was supposed to be the evolution of the 250GT series of competition berlinettas, fitted with a mid-mounted 3-litre V12 engine. However, the sport's governing body thought that Ferrari were trying to move the goalposts too far for a development of a production car and refused to sanction it as a GT car. Thus it had to race in the prototype category and was fitted with a 3.3-litre engine. Eventually it was given the all clear by the Italian national body to race as a GT in Italy. The greatest moment for this model came in 1965 when Jochen Rindt and Masten Gregory brought the NART-entered example home first ahead of the similar car of Ecurie Francorchamps in the Le Mans 24 Hour Race. The picture below shows a 250LM being raced at Silverstone in 1967 shows the similarity of line to the 1964-bodied 250GTO.

This example of a covered headlight 250GT SWB California spider is fitted with the rare optional hardtop. The Marchal driving lights in the radiator grille opening are a more common feature often seen on this model. As with the 250GT SWB berlinetta, the client could specify the state of engine tune and rear-axle ratio when ordering the car. Although they were basically a competition-model derived road car, they did get raced, notably at Le Mans in 1959, when one finished fifth overall, and in 1960 when one retired while in eleventh place with two of the twenty-four hours remaining. In the Sebring 12 Hour Race in 1959 one finished ninth and at the same race in 1960 examples finished fifth, eighth and tenth.

The public had their first view of the 250GTE, or 2+2, when it was used as the course car for the 1960 Le Mans 24 Hour Race. This was the first series production 2+2 Ferrari, although they had built a few limited production 2+2 models during the 1950s. Production started in 1960 and they were manufactured until '63, the last few of the series receiving a 4-litre engine and being called 330 Americas, but these had no external identifying features. The example seen here is one that was used by the Italian police as a high-speed pursuit car in the early 1960s – if you can't beat them, join them! In August 1963 *Autosport* magazine recorded a top speed of 136.7mph and a 0–60mph time of just over 7 seconds.

250GTE production was split into three series. Series I cars featured rear lights with separate small circular lenses in a vertical cluster with a chrome bezel and driving lights within the radiator grille recess. Series II cars had a minor change to the dasboard but were otherwise as series I cars. Series III cars had vertical one-piece rear light clusters, with the driving lights outboard of the grille, which also necessitated repositioning of the sidelights. From this description it can be seen that this is a series III model or it could be a 330 America! (See previous caption)

The replacement for the street 250GT SWB berlinetta was the 250GT Lusso model. This model had a different chassis, still with a 2,400 mm wheelbase, in which the 3-litre V12 engine was mounted further forward to provide more space in the passenger compartment. This is one of two prototype models, chassis number 4335GT, which has covered headlights and a nose style that would feature on the 330GTC of 1966. The model was first displayed at the 1962 Paris Salon and production commenced in early 1963.

The standard production version of the 250GT Lusso had open headlights, built-in driving lights outboard of the grille and an unusual three-piece front bumper arrangement. The overall balance of shape and cleanness of line is regarded by many to be one of Pininfarina's masterpieces. This was the last of the 3-litre 250 series of V12 road cars and production ceased in 1964, when the replacement 275GTB berlinetta was announced.

As in the late 1950s, the practice of producing exclusive, large-engined, low-volume production models continued through most of the 1960s, although by now the designs were virtually exclusively the province of Pininfarina. The decade started with the 400SA models, 400 referring to a 4-litre V12 engine and SA for Superamerica. The first of these models was built on chassis number 1517SA in 1959 but underwent cosmetic surgery to appear in the form seen here in 1960. Features of note on this one-off example, built for Fiat group supremo Gianni Agnelli, are the large wrap-around windscreen, the twin headlights in projecting pods and the large square radiator grille with a fine mesh, all very non-Ferrari items. It is also interesting to note that the car carries no badging, either Ferrari or Pininfarina.

Only six of these 400SA cabriolets were produced from 1960 onwards, while a single 250GT was fitted with a similar body for a French client, which is pictured from the rear earlier in this chapter (see p. 68). The family resemblance to the 250GT California spider can be seen in this view, although the radiator grille is much shallower and the tail treatment is more angular, as can be noted in the previously mentioned photograph.

The frontal treatment of this 400SA coupé is very similar to the cabriolet version of the model, however the rear-end treatment is virtually identical to the Superfast II and 1962 production 400SA coupé. Despite being a mix of two different body styles, the overall shape works very well and was necessary for Italian-market cars of the period because of lighting legislation prohibiting the use of covered headlights. Strangely this didn't stop design studies with covered lights and some of these studies actually became registered for the road in Italy. By 1962 the regulation was relaxed, thus allowing more freedom in production-car design. The example seen here is chassis number 3361SA.

This 400SA, called the Superfast II and built on chassis number 2207SA, was presented at the 1960 Turin Salon in the form seen here. In this form it was used as the personal car of Battista (Pinin) Farina, before supposedly undergoing modifications on two occasions to become the Superfast III and IV prototypes. However, it would be the Superfast II shape that would be closest to the production version of 1962.

The final definitive form of the 400SA model can be seen to have very close links with the Superfast II prototype, the main visual difference being the front wing profile, which has been altered to accommodate conventional covered headlights to replace the prototype's retractable units in the nose panel. The early cars in the 400SA series were built on a 2,400 mm wheelbase chassis, while those from January 1962 had a 2,600 mm unit, giving more space behind the seats and better straight-line stability.

It was very rare for any Ferrari to carry a model identification badge but the 400SA was one of the rare exceptions and had this chrome badge on the bootlid, positioned below the crossed shields of Ferrari and Pininfarina. It is interesting to note, also, that the Ferrari script does not have its normal elongated 'F'.

The 500 Superfast was the last of the large-engined low volume production coupés to be produced by Ferrari and was introduced at the 1964 Geneva Salon. The 500 in the model name referred to the 5-litre V12 engine specific to this model, which had triple Weber twin-choke carburettors, a single overhead camshaft per bank of cylinders and was coupled to a five-speed gearbox. The very smooth body was the work of Pininfarina on a 2,650 mm wheelbase and the resemblance to the 400SA model that it replaced is quite obvious. Only thirty-six examples were built between 1964 and '66, one of which was owned by the actor Peter Sellers.

The 365 California spider was the very last of the low-volume production Ferraris in the 1960s. It was introduced at the 1966 Geneva Salon and production continued into the middle of 1967, during which time only fourteen examples were built. The engine was 4.4-litre V12 single overhead camshaft per bank unit, with the 365 part of the model title referring to the cubic capacity of a single cylinder. The front of the Pininfarina body resembled the 500 Superfast but the tail was more angular and sharply cut off to form a flat rear panel featuring light units unique to this model. The nose panel of most examples featured retractable driving lights just inboard of the headlight cowls and the doors had a tapered scalloped indentation incorporating the handle in a central chrome strip. The tapered scalloped section would subsequently feature on the Dino and 308/328 series of cars.

The replacement for the 250GT Lusso model was the 275GTB, which was introduced at the 1964 Paris Salon. The Pininfarina-designed, Scaglietti-built body carried styling influences from the 250GTO but with greater volume to the curves. The engine is a 3.3-litre V12 single overhead camshaft per bank unit, hence the 275 model designation, which was coupled via a drive shaft running at engine speed to a five-speed transaxle, with independent rear suspension. This was the first touring Ferrari to be fitted with a transaxle and independent rear suspension.

A 275GTB two-camshaft long nose model in action.

Introduced concurrently with the 275GTB in 1964 was the 275GTS spider model. It shared the same mechanical components and layout, although with a lower state of tune engine, but as can be seen had a completely different style of body by Pininfarina, who also constructed it. The lines were more influenced by the 330GT 2+2 model than its berlinetta sister. Initially a three-seat format was proposed, the driver's seat and a broad passenger seat capable of holding two people, but it is believed that only a prototype and perhaps a few early production cars appeared in this form. The only change to the body during production was the design of the wing-side exhaust vents in 1965; seen here is a post-change model with three large slots, whereas earlier cars had eleven narrow slots. Production ceased in 1966, when the the two-camshaft engine was superceded.

Whether in action or static, the 275GTB makes a statement of power, which is probably greater with the more aggressive

short nose and larger radiator grille seen here than the smoother long nose that replaced it.

The 275GTB with two-camshaft engine in its second guise with the long nose front, introduced at the 1965 Paris Salon. The shape of the nose was changed to counteract front-end lift at high speed that had been experienced with the original short nose. Concurrent with the change to the nose was an increase in rear screen size and the adoption of

chrome external hinges for the boot lid. The example pictured here has the optional Borrani wire wheels, in place of the standard cast-aluminium ones, while the silver paintwork complements the powerful curves of the Pininfarina-designed body.

This is a competition variant on the 275GTB, of which only three were produced in this body form, constructed in lightweight aluminium by Scaglietti. This is chassis number 06885, which was raced at the 1965 Le Mans 24 Hour Race by the Belgian Ecurie Francorchamps, where it finished third overall and won the GT class, driven by Mairesse/Blaton. The influence of the 250GTO is even more pronounced than on the road car, particularly around the nose.

The more usual competition version of the 275GTB is called the 275GTB/C and is virtually identical to the normal long-nose road version. However, the body is constructed in light aluminium and there are subtle differences in dimensions that are almost undetectable, as presumably they were supposed to be in order to comply with the regulations. Even the bumpers were very light units mounted straight on to the body rather than to bumper irons fixed to the chassis. All C examples had two camshaft engines and a total of twelve cars were built to this specification during 1966.

The 275GTB/4 was the final evolution of the 275 series, with the main difference being the new four-camshaft (two per bank) version of the 3.3-litre V12 engine. This was the first production-Ferrari road car to be fitted with a four-camshaft V12 engine, which raised power output by over 25 bhp compared to the two-camshaft unit. Visually the four-camshaft cars can be identified by the raised centre section on the bonnet. Below is a further example of a two-camshaft special competition derivative, chassis number 06701, which when compared with the similar example at the top of page 88, has several detail differences.

At the instigation of Luigi Chinetti, the then Ferrari importer for the USA, a small series of open versions of the four-camshaft 275GTB was built, called the 275GTB/4S NART Spider. Strangely, sales were slow and only ten examples were ever constructed, although in recent years it has become one of the most sought-after models by Ferrari collectors, and a number of berlinettas (both two- and four-camshaft versions) have been converted to this form.

The 330GT 2+2 was introduced in January 1964 as a replacement for the 250 GTE model. Like its predecessor, the number in the model title referred to the cubic capacity of a single cylinder, hence the total capacity of the V12 engine was 4 litres. The body was the work of Pininfarina and it was the first series production Ferrari to have twin headlights, which in their angled chrome surrounds gave the front quite an aggressive stance. At about this time wire wheels, which had been *de rigeur* on sports and GT cars, were starting to be replaced by cast light-aluminium wheels and the 330GT 2+2 was the last Ferrari model to have them fitted as standard equipment, although they were still available as an option on later models.

Even the more 'staid' 2+2 examples get occasional competition use, as with this 330GT 2+2 S1 at Silverstone in 1979.

In the middle of 1965 the 330GT 2+2 had a facelift which resulted in the introduction of the Series II model. The most obvious difference is the deletion of the twin headlight arrangement in favour of a more conservative single unit, with revised sidelight/indicator assemblies below them. The family resemblance to the 275GTS model is evident in this view. The gearbox was changed from a four-speed plus overdrive to a five-speed unit and the design of the exhaust outlet on each front wing side was changed, in the same way that it had been on the 275GTS. The standard road wheels became cast aluminium but kept the familiar three-eared knock-off central retaining nut.

Vignale's last Ferrari offering was this station wagon, based on a 330GT 2+2, chassis number 7963, which was presented at the 1968 Turin Salon. It was finished in metallic green with a gold roof and the standard model's cast-aluminium wheels were retained. The car was built at the wish of the son of the then American Ferrari importer, Luigi Chinetti, and it remained in the USA for many years before returning to Europe in the mid-1990s.

The next model to be introduced in the 330 series was the two-seater 330GTC coupé, which was presented at the 1966 Geneva Salon. The front section bore a similarity to the 500 Superfast in general design, while the rear was very similar to the 275GTS. The passenger compartment featured a large glass area with very slim screen pillars, which provided excellent all-round visibility. The front wings carried exhaust outlets identical to those on the 275GTS and 330GT 2+2. This model was fitted with a five-speed transaxle, as on the 275GTB, but featured an enclosed drive shaft from the engine, which was also then adopted on the 275GTB. This example features the standard cast-aluminium wheels.

Following close on the heels of the coupé model came the 330GTS spider model, the C in the 330GTC and the S in the 330GTS referring to either coupé or spider. The official presentation of this model was at the 1968 Paris Salon. Apart from the folding canvas roof, the spider is visually identical to the coupé version. Production of both cars continued into late 1968, when they were superceded by the 365GTC/S models.

Pininfarina were still producing the occasional custom-built car for special clients based on a production chassis. One of the last of these projects during the 1960s was a pair of identical 330GTCs built in 1967 on chassis numbers 09439 and 09653, the former being for Princess Liliane de Rethy. Although there are similarities in shape at the front with a standard 330GTC, where the nose panel features retractable lights as on the 365 California, the cabin and rear section are completely different and carried features that would appear in future production models.

The 365GTC was announced in late 1968 as the replacement for the 330GTC, which it is visually very similar to. The only external distinguishing feature between the two models is the deletion of the wing-side exhaust vents on the 365GTC, which were superceded by a pair of rectangular black grilles towards the rear edge of the bonnet. An example of this model was road tested by *Autocar* magazine in 1969 and a mean maximum speed of 151mph and a 0–100mph time of 14.7 seconds were recorded. To put this performance into context, a Jaguar 'E' Type with a similar engine capacity, and recorded by the same magazine in that period, reached 140mph and required 17.1 seconds to reach the magic 100mph.

The spider version bore the same differences as the coupé to its predecessor, with the 365 designation in the model title of both GTC and GTS models relating to the increased engine capacity, which was now 4.4 litres. Both the 365GTS, seen here, and the 365GTC above are fitted with the optional wire wheels.

Although Ferrari were still some time away from a production mid-engined twelve-cylinder car, the mid-engined V6 Dino was being developed, and from those designs Pininfarina created this mid-engined twelve-cylinder offering at the Paris Salon in 1966, called the 365P. This example is chassis number 08971, while a second model was built on chassis number 08815 for Fiat supremo Gianni Agnelli, which featured a brushed stainless-steel tail spoiler. One of the more unusual aspects of these cars was their central driving position, with a passenger seat set back on either side of the driver, a feature that appeared on the McLaren Formula 1 road car in the 1990s.

The original wooden body buck for the 365P of 1966, seen here at L'Idea Ferrari exhibition held at the Forte di Belvedere in Florence during the summer of 1990. This concept of building a master mould in wood was part of the coachbuilder's tradition and the idea is still in use today, although the materials differ.

The replacement 2+2 model for the 330GT 2+2 was the 365GT 2+2, affectionately nicknamed the 'Queen Mary' by Ferrari enthusiasts due to its length, even though it shared a 2,650 mm wheelbase with its predecessor. The family resemblance to other models of the period is clear, while the rear side glass shape and tail treatment resemble the pair of special 330GTCs built in 1967 (see p. 93). This model was introduced in late 1967 and continued in production until early 1971. It was the first Ferrari to have power steering as standard and also featured hydraulically operated self-levelling rear suspension.

Some of the sales brochures for various models from the 1960s.

Chapter 4

FIAT MOVES IN

The Ferrari/Fiat alliance gave birth to the Dino range of cars, the first prototype of which was exhibited by Pininfarina at the 1965 Paris Salon. This was built on a Dino sports racing car, chassis number 0840, and featured the longitudinal mid-engine placement of that model. Even at this early stage in the development, the basic parameters of the model shape are in place: the bulbous front wings, curved rear window glass, scalloped door intakes and sharply cut off tail panel.

Introduction

During the early 1960s Ford of America had courted Ferrari and almost reached an agreement to purchase the company, but ultimately this came to nothing.. This led to Ford entering motor racing independently with the legendary GT40 sports racing car and determined to beat Ferrari in the prestigious World Sports Car Championship. The first alliance between Ferrari and Fiat came in 1965 when motor sport's governing body, the FISA (Federatione Internationale Sport Automobile), announced that from 1967 all Formula 2 cars would have to be fitted with a production-based engine with a minimum annual output of 500 units. This was beyond Ferrari's capacity and led them to Fiat's door, where an agreement was reached whereby Fiat would manufacture a Ferrari-designed 2-litre V6 engine for use in Fiat cars carrying the Dino badge and a new small Ferrari that would be built under the Dino name. This arrangement provided Ferrari with a production-based engine for the Formula 2 cars and Fiat with the cachet of the Dino/Ferrari involvement on their sports models, the Pininfarina-designed Fiat Dino spider and the Bertone-designed Fiat Dino coupé.

The Ford onslaught in sports-car racing, together with their involvement in 1967 with Cosworth Engineering to produce the immediately competitive Ford Cosworth DFV V8 Formula 1 engine, resulted in Ferrari having to spend more and more money on their racing efforts in order to remain in the hunt. This proved to be an increasing drain on their resources and in 1969 resulted in another knock on Fiat's door, where Enzo Ferrari caught the sympathetic ear of the Fiat president, Gianni Agnelli, and a deal was concluded. Fiat would purchase 50 per cent of the Ferrari production-car business and receive a further 40 per cent on the death of Enzo Ferrari, who maintained complete control of the racing division. This agreement suited Enzo Ferrari as it reduced his activities on the production-car side and allowed him to concentrate his energies on his first love, the racing department.

There were no radical changes when the new Fiat management team took office at Ferrari during 1969. The Dino model received a larger engine and became the 246GT and continued in this form with minor modifications and the addition of a targa-topped variant, the 246GTS, in 1972, until production ceased in 1974. The 246 Dinos were the first Ferraris to receive pressed steel body panels, that were pressed at the Pininfarina factory in Turin, followed by body assembly at the Scaglietti works in Modena, before being transported to the Ferrari factory for mechanical assembly. The first totally new, post-Fiat model to be introduced was the 365GTC/4, nominally a 2+2 that replaced the 365 GTC and the 365GT 2+2 in 1971. Also introduced in 1971 was a version of the 365GTB/4 aimed at the USA market, which in the interests of production uniformity resulted in all versions of the model receiving a retractable headlight arrangement, necessary to satisfy USA legislation at that time. The proposed replacement for the 365GTB/4 Daytona was presented at the 1971 Turin Salon and pointed the way for the future. This was the 365GT4/BB, a mid-engined flat-twelve design with a distinctive wedge profile that was very much in vogue at the time and, it almost goes without saying, was penned by Pininfarina. This brought Ferrari into line with Lamborghini, who had introduced the mid-engined Bertone-designed Muira at the 1966 Geneva Salon, although a rolling chassis without body was shown the previous year. It also matched Maserati, who had introduced their mid-engined offering, the Bora, at the 1971 Geneva Salon.

By 1970 Ferrari employed a thousand people and the production total was approaching that figure with 928 cars produced, including the separately badged Dinos. The 1,000 cars per annum milestone was reached the following year when a total of 1,246 cars rolled out of the factory gates. The Fiat-trained management team were striking the right balance between maintaining the exclusivity of the marque, updating production techniques and equipment to maximize operating efficiency, while retaining a degree of artisan, hand-built craftsmanship in the product.

The next Dino prototype, shown at the Turin Salon in 1966, resembled the final production model even more closely, with the headlights moved into the wings and the shallow elliptical radiator grille shape almost in its production form. The first prototype had no radiator grille, but instead a full-width Plexiglas cover housing the headlight assemblies mounted in the nose. The rear light arrangement on this second prototype, chassis number 00106 – the first in a special Dino sequence – is identical to that on the 365P prototypes of the same era. This prototype also featured the five-spoke 'star' wheels that were to become a Ferrari hallmark for many years; even the wheels on the current production models are a development of that theme.

After the Dino prototype phase, the first model went into production in 1968 – the 206GT, thus named because of its 2-litre V6 cylinder engine. The engine was transversely mid-mounted in unit with the five-speed gearbox and final drive assembly, leaving space for a reasonable luggage compartment in the tail of the car. Although a 206GT has a different wheelbase to the later 246GT, this is not perceptible and the most obvious identifying feature is the exposed fuel filler cap on the left sail panel. Production of the 206GT only lasted into early 1969 when the 246GT replaced it, by which time only about 150 examples had been built, all of which were left-hand drive. The complete Dino series had their own even-number chassis sequence range.

A 206GT being exercised during a Ferrari Club meeting in the mountains near Maranello, the birthplace of Ferrari cars.

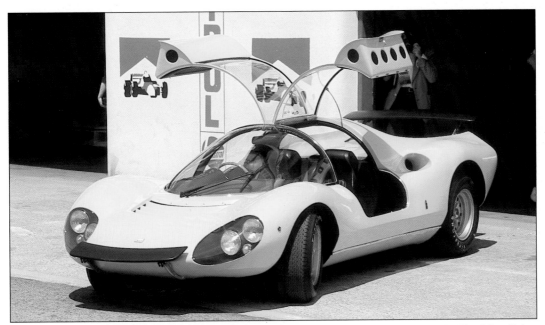

A Pininfarina styling exercise for a competition derivative of the Dino was shown at the Frankfurt Salon in 1967. Built on a 206S competition chassis number 034, it was intended as a study in aerodynamic solutions for the competition car. For many years it was thought that it was only a static show car but it came out of the Pininfarina museum in the late 1980s for a large Ferrari gathering at the Imola circuit and proved that it was a fully operational automobile.

When the Dino engine size was increased to 2.4 litres the model name, 246GT, reflected the change and at the same time the engine block became cast iron instead of silumin alloy. The body also changed from aluminium to steel, albeit with some aluminium panels. Visually the most obvious difference was the provision of a cover over the fuel filler on the left sail panel. Early 246GT models still had the knock-off spinner wheel fixing but this soon changed to a five-bolt retaining system. A spider model, the 246GTS, with a removable targa top, was introduced at the Geneva Salon in 1972, both models of the 246GT being available in right- and left-hand drive and a USA market model featuring ugly rectangular marker lights in the wing sides was also made. The Dino was supposed to be a marque in its own right and no Ferrari badges were ever fitted to them at the factory, although many examples now carry them, as with the car seen here.

The 365GTB/4 Daytona was the replacement for the 275GTB/4 model and was introduced at the 1968 Paris Salon. The prototype had featured a frontal treatment similar to the 275GTB/4 but by the time it made its public debut this had been changed to the wedge nose with twin headlights under a full-width Plexiglas cover, as seen here. This model set new performance standards for its time and for many years held the record as the fastest car ever road tested by the magazine *Autocar*, reaching a mean top speed of 174mph and attaining 0–100mph in 12.6 seconds.

Pininfarina produced this one-off coupé design study on the 365GTB/4 for the 1969 Paris Salon, featuring a brushed stainless-steel roll hoop and a removable rear window. The bumpers also extend further around the body sides on this example. The American importer, Luigi Chinetti, commissioned three special-bodied examples from Michelotti after production had finished in 1974, one of which was bought by the actor Steve McQueen, although they bear no resemblance to a standard Daytona. A further example was rebodied by Panther Westwinds of Byfleet, Surrey, in the late 1970s as a station wagon.

Because of USA market lighting legislation the 365GTB/4 headlight arrangement was changed from the covered lights to twin retractable units in the middle of 1971, the new arrangement having only a minimal effect on the appearance of the car. The large orange indicator lights on the front corners feature a circular reflector on the side incorporating the Cavallino Rampante. Cars produced for the USA market had rectangular side marker lights cut into the rear wings.

This 365GTB/4, seen rounding Druids Hill bend at Brands Hatch during a test day, is fitted with the optional Borrani wire wheels and 'cigarette packet' sidelights on the top outer quarter bumper edges.

The 365GTB/4 Daytona was also raced with quite a degree of success in the GT class by private and concessionaire teams, fifteen of these cars being built up at the Ferrari Assistenza Tecnica Workshop in Modena. They gained the suffix C for *competizione*, to become 365GTB/4Cs. The bodies were constructed from aluminium and the engines provided with different

profile camshafts, a higher compression ratio, with careful balancing and other modifications eventually producing a 100bhp power increase over the standard road car. This is the ex-Maranello Concessionaire's team car in their red and Cambridge blue livery, chassis number 15681.

At the 1969 Frankfurt Salon a spider version of the Daytona, the 3656TB/4S, was introduced, which was produced alongside the coupé until production of both models ceased in 1973. During that time they accounted for about 10 per cent of the total Daytona production and most were USA market versions. Since then a number of coupés have been converted to spider form, mainly in the USA and England. The majority of these conversions are very professional and the only way to be totally sure if a car is a genuine example is to check the chassis number against the factory build-sheet details.

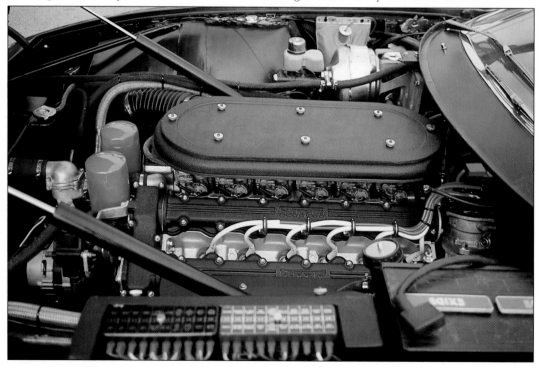

The packed engine bay of the 365GTB/4 Daytona is dominated by the vast black crackle-paint-finished air cleaner, with the twin oil filters just ahead of it. In the foreground is the fusebox and battery, with the left twin camshaft cover visible between them and the air filter.

The 365GTC/4 was introduced as a replacement for the 365GTC at the 1971 Geneva Salon but with a marginal 2+2 seating arrangement, which meant that it would also to a degree fill the gap left by the 365GT 2+2 model. The engine was basically the same unit as fitted to the 365GTB/4 but with a lower compression ratio and triple side-draught twin-choke carburettors per bank of cylinders, instead of the bank of six downdraught carburettors in the centre of the vee on the 365GTB/4. The five-speed gearbox was in unit with the engine, whereas the 365GTB/4 Daytona used a five-speed transaxle. Production continued until the late summer of 1972.

The 365GT4/BB, the 'BB' standing for berlinetta boxer, with the 'boxer' part of the name referring to the firing sequence of the flat-twelve engine. The Ferrari flat-twelve racing engines were true boxer engines in that the opposite pistons on the crankshaft moved together and away at the same time. On this production engine one piston moved away as the other approached, so there was a degree of artistic licence in the name. The engine used the same bore and stroke as the Daytona but, as already stated, was a flat twelve constructed in unit with the gearbox and final drive and was mid-mounted longitudinally. The model was first presented at the 1971 Turin Salon but did not go into production until 1973, alongside the 365GTB/4 Daytona. Perhaps Ferrari wanted to gauge client reaction to the mid-engine concept before dropping the front-engined model.

Enthusiastic owners used their road cars in national level club racing, more for the enjoyment of competition than for a realistic chance of winning. This obviously well-used 365GT4/BB is being pushed hard around Druids Hill bend at Brands Hatch.

This rear view of a 365GT4/BB shows the triple rear-light arrangement each side, which matches the exhaust tailpipe treatment below. The rear panel between the lights is mesh, which changed to louvres on the larger-engined 512 versions of the model.

Chapter 5

THE MID-ENGINED ERA

At the Paris Salon in 1976 a revised berlinetta boxer was introduced called the BB512, the model name being much simplified with the number 5 referring to the total cubic capacity in litres and 12 for the number of cylinders. Apart from the increase in engine capacity, there were modifications to the bodywork. The most noticeable were the deep front spoiler below the radiator grille at the front, NACA intakes on the lower body sides to duct cool air to the rear brakes, a revised rear-light arrangement of two large circular units per side replacing the triple units and a twin large-bore tailpipe per side exhaust system, again replacing the triple small-bore outlets of the earlier model. The larger engine produced slightly less power than the previous unit but it had far greater torque, making it much more user friendly.

Introduction

The mid-engined concept had been with Ferrari since 1961, when the 'Shark Nose' 156 Formula 1 car was announced following the design leads of the British Cooper and Lotus concerns. This design philosophy was transferred to the sports racing models with the similarly nosed 246S sports racing model the same year. The first mid-engined GT car was supposed to have been the 250LM in 1963, which was produced with road-car sequence odd chassis numbers, but the FIA refused to recognize it as a development of the 250 series of road cars and thus it could not compete in the GT class. The next step was the 1965 Dino prototype, followed by the 365P in 1966, which featured three seats with a central driving position, an idea recently resurrected by McLaren on their Formula 1 road car, then the production Dinos and the 365GT4/BB shown at the 1971 Turin Salon. This model took a further two years to reach the production line, the first examples being delivered in 1973 just at the time when the oil crisis caused an escalation of petrol prices and made such machines social misfits. Although it was reported that Ferrari had plenty of advance orders for the new top of the range model, the car that it was replacing, the 365GTB/4 Daytona, continued in production alongside it during 1973. The mid-engine emphasis in the range was expanded with the introduction of the Dino 308GT4 in 1973, a 2+2 addition to the Dino stable, again following the fashionable wedge styling, this time from the pen of Bertone. It was termed wedge styling because of the mainly flat panels with sharp angles that produced a low front gradually getting deeper to the cockpit, hence the resemblance to a door wedge. This was the only series production Ferrari designed by anyone other than Pininfarina and initially received a lukewarm reception from the press because of its appearance, which was thought to be rather bland in comparison with the stunning 246 Dino. However, in reality Bertone had done a very effective job of packaging a 2+2 seating arrangement into a well-balanced overall shape. This was born out when the Pininfarina-designed replacement, the Mondial 8, was announced in 1980, which was larger all round and didn't have the same tight fluid lines of the GT4.

When the 246 Dino went out of production in 1974 there was no small capacity two-seater in the range until the first fibreglass-bodied production Ferrari, the 308GTB, was presented in 1976. Although it was wedge shaped there were styling cues from the late-lamented 246 Dino and it won instant approval from clients and press alike. The Dino name had been dropped as a marque in its own entity in 1975 at the behest of American dealers. They had a hard time selling the Dino 308GT4 (which was then the only Ferrari on the American market because of emission legislation and didn't even carry a Ferrari badge!) and therefore it was rebadged as a Ferrari and Dino 308GT4 became the model name.

The only model in the range to maintain the classic front engine with rear-wheel-drive configuration was the 365GT4 2+2 model, introduced in late 1972, and which was effectively a lengthened and restyled 365GTC/4. This evolved into the 400 series, the first model on which Ferrari offered automatic transmission, and finally the 412 model which ceased production in 1989. The overall shape only underwent minor changes to detail during the seventeen years that the variants of the model were in production. There was then a three-year period when Ferrari had no large capacity 2+2 model in the range, remedied in 1992 when the 456GT was introduced, initially only with a six-speed manual gearbox and then from 1996 with the option of an automatic gearbox.

By the mid-1970s the bulk of Ferrari production cars were mid-engined and the majority of these were of V8 configuration. The 308GTB changed to a steel/aluminium body construction after a short while and was joined by a targa-topped variant, the 308GTS, in 1977; they gained fuel injection in 1980 and four valves per cylinder in 1982. A body facelift and increased engine capacity in 1986 created the 328GTB/S models. These were replaced in 1989 by the 348 series, which in appearance was reminiscent of the top of the range Testarossa model. A full convertible called the 348 spider joined the two-seater V8 range in 1993. The 348 models were replaced by the F355 series in 1994, although the 348 spider version continued into 1995 alongside the F355s. During the 1980s two limited production run V8 models were produced. In 1984 the 288GTO was announced, with a twin-turbo, longitudinally mounted V8 engine, with fatter wheel arches and bigger spoilers, which made it look like a 308GTB on steroids. An even more radical model was presented in 1987 to mark the fortieth anniversary of Ferrari production – the winged wonder called the F40, a real racing car for the road.

The 2+2 mid-engined V8 coupé theme that started with the Dino 308GT4 in 1973 continued with the Mondial 8 in 1980, which was the first production Ferrari to be fitted with fuel injection from new. In 1982 it received the four-valve per cylinder engine and a cabriolet version joined the range. The engine capacity was increased to 3.2 litres in 1986 and in 1989 the longitudinal engine placement of the 348 series was adopted along with the transverse gearbox of that model to provide the final model in the series, the Mondial t, which was slowly phased out of production during 1993. Between 1975 and 1989 Ferrari also produced 2-litre engined variants of some models specifically for the Italian market, where taxes are punitive on any car over that engine capacity.

At the top of the range the flat-twelve engine dominated for more than two decades. The 365GT4/BB was developed into the 512BB in 1976, which received fuel injection in 1981 to become the 512BBi. The Testarossa replaced this model in 1984, a model easily identifiable by its vast girth and deeply slatted radiator intake ducts in the doors. Facelifts saw this model become the 512TR and then the F512M before production ceased in 1996. The next top of the range two seater would see a return to a front-engined, rear-wheel-drive layout.

A further limited production model, probably the final one of the century, was presented at the 1995 Geneva Salon. Even wilder than the F40 in appearance, and dubbed the Formula 1 car for the road, this was the V12-engined F50 which had an engine derived from that used in the 1990 Formula 1 car.

The final evolution of the berlinetta boxer came in 1981 when it was provided with Bosch K Jetronic fuel injection in place of the four triple-choke Weber carburettors. The most obvious differences between a BB512 and BB512i are the revised radiator grille on the i (injection) model, which incorporates driving lights in the extremities with small rectangular sidelights in the bumper above them.

A BB512i from the rear, where a further difference to the BB512 can be seen: the provision of high-intensity fog lights outboard of the exhaust tailpipes in the exhaust shroud. The BB512i continued in production until 1984 but because of further USA legislation controlling emissions, Ferrari never produced a version for that market.

As with the 36567B/4 Daytona, it was the American Ferrari importer, Luigi Chinetti, who introduced the berlinetta boxer to competition when he prepared a 365GT4/BB, chassis number 18095, for the 1975 season. This car started as a lightly modified road car but was gradually developed over the next two years and was eventually fitted with a 5-litre engine. This exercise prompted the French and Belgian importers to prepare cars for the Le Mans 24 Hour Race in 1978. The next evolution was wind-tunnel studies by Pininfarina which resulted in radically different bodywork for a series of cars built at Ferrari's Assistenza Tecnica in Modena during 1979. These were given the name 512BB/LM, the LM referring to Le Mans, which was the race that they had primarily been built for. Between 1980 and '82 a second series of these cars was built, one of which is seen here, that differed slightly in body detail from the first series of 1979. The main visible differences are the profile of the brake cooling intakes on the rear wings and the shape of the sill section between the front and rear wheels.

In 1980 Pininfarina produced a design study for a four-door full-four-seat (as opposed to the previous 2+2) Ferrari to mark their fiftieth anniversary, which they called the Pinin. The car was fitted with the 5-litre flat-twelve engine of the berlinetta boxer mounted at the front, although it never developed beyond the prototype stage. The use of aerodynamic spokes on the road wheels would be used again, in modified form, on the 348 series and F512M, while some details were used on other Pininfarina designs, such as the narrow full-length body side crease that featured on the Alfa Romeo 164 and Peugeot 405.

The Testarossa had its press launch at the Lido Nightclub on the Champs-Elysée in Paris on the eve of the 1984 Paris Salon. It was vastly different in appearance to the 512BBi that it replaced, due mainly to the side-mounted water radiators that necessitated large slatted cooling ducts in the door panels. This added considerable girth to the car, the rear wheelbase being increased by nearly 100 mm. The engine layout was very similar to that of its predecessor but it had four valves per cylinder heads, which together with other modifications produced a further 50bhp. The model name Testarossa was a derivation of Testa Rossa, used on the sports racing models of the 1950s, and the new car had the cam covers painted red in the old tradition. Initially there was a single driver's door mirror mounted halfway up the screen pillar but this changed to the twin arrangement seen here, although strangely the catalogue for the model always featured the original layout throughout the seven-year production run. The early models also had the wheels retained by a single central nut but this was changed to a standard five-bolt fixing on later cars.

The first facelift on the Testarossa came with the 1992 model year when the 512TR was announced. The model name reflected a return to a description by engine size and form: the 512TR, meaning a 5-litre twelve-cylinder engine and 'TR' being an abbreviation for Testa Rossa. Visually the differences were a new design of road wheel, which had five slimmer curved spokes, and a revised front panel and auxilliary light arrangement that was similar to the 348 models introduced in 1989.

The final evolution of the flat-twelve mid-engined series was presented at the 1994 Paris Salon and bore the model title F512M, F for Ferrari and M for *modificato* (modified). The new model had a heavily revised interior, the retractable headlights of the previous models were replaced by homofocal units under glass covers, the front panel design changed to a design similar to the recently introduced F355 model and small NACA ducts provided in the bonnet for better interior ventilation. The road wheels featured aerofoil spokes and split rims and the tail lost its distinctive full-width grille over the lights, replaced by uncovered paired circular light units on each side with a small grille between them.

The heart of the Testarossa, the 5-litre flat-twelve engine, seen here in cut-away form while on display in the Ferrari factory reception area. The red painted camshaft cover to the right bank of cylinders is clearly visible, as are the beautiful cast-aluminium intake plenums and induction manifolds for the fuel injection system on top of the engine.

After eighteen months without a true 2+2 model in the range the 365GT4 2+2 was introduced at the Paris Salon in 1972. The body was a very elegant, classically conservative design from Pininfarina which featured a large glass area to provide an airy interior and good visibility. The interior had sumptuously upholstered leather seats to provide armchair-like comfort for the occupants. The 365GT4 2+2 can most easily be identified from later models by the triple circular rear-light arrangement, similar to that on the 365GTC/4 and 365GT4/BB, and the knock-off central wheel-retaining nut. The subsequent 400 series cars had a larger twin-lense arrangement and five-bolt wheel fixing. This model continued in production until 1976.

The 400 series was introduced at the 1976 Paris Salon and was the first Ferrari to be offered with automatic transmission as standard equipment. The models were initially called the 400 Automatic and 400GT (fitted with a five-speed manual gearbox), and became the 400i Automatic and 400iGT when fuel injection was introduced in 1979. The automatic transmission found favour with the majority of buyers and examples with manual gearboxes are now much more difficult to find. The 400 in the model title reflected the cubic capacity of a single cylinder, hence it had a total cubic capacity of 4.8 litres. There were small changes to the radiator grille arrangement during the life of the series, with the driving lights initially being behind the grille and then later, as seen on this 400i, they were uncovered in the grille extremities.

The rear view of a 400i can be compared with that of the 365GT4 2+2 – the lighting arrangement differences are obvious (see p. 116). The 400 series continued in production for nearly nine years with very few changes to the overall design.

For the Geneva show in 1985 the 400 series underwent a facelift to become the 412 model, again available with either manual or automatic transmission. This was the first Ferrari to be offered with an ABS braking system. The 412 model title reflected an increase in engine size to 5 litres, while bodily the most obvious differences are a change in road wheel design, the body colour-coded bumpers and a raising of the rear wing line and boot lid to provide greater space within the latter. The 412 series ceased production in 1989.

A number of 400/412 series cars have been modified to convertibles over the years, particularly during the 1980s when these conversions seemed to have been in vogue. The example seen here is the only one built by Ferrari as a full convertible as a design and viability study on a 412, chassis number 73011. After the factory had finished their studies the car went to Motor Service SRL, the concessionaire in Modena, who completed the unfinished project car.

The introduction of the Dino 308GT4 in 1973 witnessed a major deviation from Ferrari policy in that Pininfarina was not the designer of the car. The brief had been given to Bertone, who came up with a very fashionable wedge-shaped 2+2 addition to the Dino range. The car was not well received initially because, in comparison to the two-seater Dino 246GT, it was considered very plain. However, Bertone had produced a very tight package that worked well considering the design brief he was given, in particular the mid-engine layout and maximum wheelbase. Early cars were badged as Dinos, as with the example seen in this Bertone publicity shot, and had the driving lights outboard of the radiator grille. This was the first production Ferrari to be fitted with a V8 engine and the model name reflected the 3-litre engine capacity and eight-cylinder configuration.

A 2-litre engined version of the car called the Dino 208GT4 was produced solely for the Italian market and not sold elsewhere. This was due to the exorbitant taxes levied on owners of cars with an engine capacity above 2 litres, which meant that many people wouldn't consider buying a car with a larger engine even if it was a Ferrari. This model can be identified by a lack of driving lights either side of the grille. Cars for the American market were also produced without these lights but they featured much heavier bumper assemblies, front and rear, to satisfy safety legislation in the USA. All 208GT4s and 308GT4s continued with the particular Dino even-chassis-number sequence.

In 1975 the radiator grille arrangement was changed to a full-width unit, with the driving lights behind it, and the Dino badges were replaced by Ferrari ones. In fact some earlier cars, particularly in the USA, had Ferrari badges fitted by the dealers to a factory instruction to try and boost sales. Early cars had road wheels similar to the Dino 246GT, except they had a small hubcap covering the wheel nuts which was later changed to an exposed nut layout. Wider five-spoke wheels, as fitted to the car seen here, were available as an option. Despite the initial criticism, the model is now regarded as one of the best handling of the 308 series of models and in 1980 the magazine *Autocar* recorded a mean maximum speed of 154mph, with a 0–60mph time of 6.9 seconds.

The two-seater replacement for the Dino 246GT was announced at the Paris Salon in 1975, with Ferrari returning to Pininfarina for the design which pleased enthusiasts and clients. The model featured elements reminiscent of the much-loved Dino in its shape, notably the door scallops and curved rear screen. The engine and transmission assembly was exactly the same as in the 308GT4, while the body was another deparure for Ferrari as it was constructed in fibreglass by Scaglietti. The fibreglass construction was succeeded by steel in late 1976/early 1977 depending on the market and fibreglass-bodied cars can be identified by a join line across the top corner of the windscreen pillar.

A targa-roofed version called the 308GTS was introduced at the 1977 Frankfurt Salon. Apart from the removable roof section, they can be identified by the hinged black grilles over the rear quarterlights, both of these features are clearly evident in this profile view.

An option that was very popular on the 308GTB/S was the deep front spoiler, which gave the frontal aspect a more aggressive stance. Although they were the successors to the Dino, the two-seater 308 series cars were numbered in the mainstream Ferrari (at that time odd) chassis-number sequence. Initially European market cars had dry sump lubrication, with USA market cars having a wet sump system, but with the introduction of the GTS model in 1977 all market cars became wet sump.

This is the engine bay of a fuel-injection model, the 308GTBi/Si, that was introduced in 1980 to meet increasing emission legislation, particularly in the USA. The system caused a reduction in power output that affected sales, mainly in the important American market where the engine was being virtually strangled by emission-control devices.

The solution to the problem of the fall in power output was announced in 1982, with the introduction of the 308QV (*quattro valvole* – four valve) models. The new four-valve per cylinder heads coupled to the Bosch K Jetronic fuel-injection system and Marelli Digiplex ignition system restored the power output to a healthier 240bhp on European market cars, 25bhp more than the previous fuel-injected models. The QV models can be identified by a different grille arrangement with uncovered driving lights in the extremities, different door mirrors, a louvre panel across the bonnet and a different design of five-spoke wheel.

When the 208GT4 ceased production for the Italian market in 1980 a 2-litre version of the world market 308GTB/S was introduced, called the 208GTB/S which, apart from the tail badge, was virtually identical to the 308 series cars. In 1982 Ferrari offered a more powerful replacement at the Turin Salon – the 208 GTB/S Turbo seen here, which was again only available on the Italian market. This model can be identified by the additional slots under the radiator grille, the matt-black painted louvre panel on the bonnet, the NACA duct on the body sides forward of the rear wheel arch and a split rear bumper with exhaust grille between and shrouded exhaust pipes. The KKK turbocharger actually made this model faster than the 1980 308 GTB/S fuel-injected models.

Ferrari's next turbocharged road car was made available to the world market, albeit in very limited quantities and only in red. This was the star and sensation of the 1984 Geneva Salon, the first of the 'Supercars', the 288GTO. In appearance it was similar to a 308GTB on steroids, with fuller wheel arches, a deep front spoiler incorporating four additional driving lights, door mirrors on tall stalks and a tail spoiler to complete the image. Underneath the skin there was experimentation with composite materials and an all-new longitudinally mounted 2.85-litre V8 engine with twin turbochargers and intercoolers. The package provided breathtaking performance for a select few clients.

The engine of the 288GTO that provides the performance is dominated by the pair of intercooler radiators with the turbocharger wastegate to the rear of the crossmember, while the red-painted injection castings atop the engine nestle under the rear bulkhead. The factory claimed performance figures were a maximum speed of 189.5 mph, acceleration from 0–100kph (62.5mph) in 4.9 seconds and 0–200kph in 15.2 seconds.

In September 1985 Ferrari introduced the 308 series replacement at the Frankfurt Salon – the 328 model which, like its predecessor, was available in GTB and GTS forms. The new model had a 3.2-litre V8 engine, hence the change in model title, and while the overall body shape was very similar to the 308 models, the nose and tail had been redesigned to provide a softening of the wedge profile and a greater fluidity of line with the body colour-coded bumpers. The five-star spoked road wheel design was also changed to a mildly concave pattern and the interior was comprehensively updated.

The convex road wheels on this 328GTB indicate that it is a model with the ABS braking system, which became available as an option in 1988 and was then made standard equipment on the remainder of the series. This example also has the popular optional rear-roof spoiler that was available for both 308 and 328 models. When the magazine *Autocar* tested a 328GTB in 1987 they recorded a mean top speed of 153mph and a 0–60mph acceleration time of 5.5 seconds.

In April 1986 the replacement for the Italian market 208GTB/S Turbo was announced at the Turin Salon and was labelled simply as the GTB/S Turbo. The body was similar to that of the world market 328 models but featured a NACA duct on the body side forward of each rear wheel arch, a raised centre section to the engine cover which contained additional louvres, a series of five exhaust slots in the rear bumper and a rear-roof spoiler, which was standard equipment. The 2-litre V8 engine was fitted with a Japanese IHI turbocharger fed through a Behr intercooler to produce 254bhp at 6500rpm, which was 34bhp greater than its predecessor.

The Mondial 8 was announced at the 1980 Geneva Salon as the replacement for the 308GT4 2+2 model and was the first production Ferrari to have fuel injection as standard equipment from new. The wheelbase was 100 mm longer than the GT4 providing more space in the passenger compartment but obviously creating a weight penalty which, allied to the effect that the original fuel-injection system had on power output resulted in a somewhat disappointing performance by Ferrari standards, with a top speed some 10mph less than its predecessor. The appearance didn't gain many admirers; although in profile it was quite smooth, the heavy black plastic front and rear bumpers spoiled the overall lines and the large trapezoidal intakes on the rear wings broke up the smooth flanks. The Mondial received the four-valve per cylinder heads at the same time as the 308 models in 1982 to become the Mondial quattrovalvole, which helped boost the performance to a more acceptable level in the eyes of the press and the clients. The external appearance didn't alter apart from the tail badge. In 1983 a full cabriolet version was introduced, the roof of which echoed that of the coupé when erected.

When the Mondial received the 3.2-litre engine it was given a much appreciated facelift to become the Mondial 3.2, seen here in cabriolet form. This brought the appearance, both front and rear, more into line with its 328 cousins and, as can be seen, cleaned up the lines with the removal of the black bumpers. The wheel design also changed on this model to a smoother convex profile five-spoke design that permitted the installation of the optional ABS braking system.

From the rear the Mondial 3.2 cabriolet with the hood down has generally smooth lines, although the large trapezoidal intake on the rear wing still detracts from the cleanliness of line.

The final evolution of the Mondial series was the Mondial t, seen here in cabriolet form, which was announced in 1989. It was virtually identical in appearance to the Mondial 3.2 but at long last the trapezoidal intakes had been replaced by much smaller and neater rectangular units. Not quite as apparent are the reprofiled front and rear wings that were more bulbous than on the earlier models. However, the biggest difference on the new model was in the engine compartment, where the transverse engine placement had been abandoned in place of a new longitudinally mounted 3.4-litre V8 engine mated to a transverse gearbox, hence the t in the model title.

This one-off Mondial 3.2 was produced on chassis number 76390 for the PPG Paint Company to a design from the IDEA Studio in Turin. It was used in the USA as the 'pace car' in the 1988 Indy Cart Racing Series that was sponsored by PPG.

In the late 1980s Ferrari worked on the possibility of producing a four-wheel drive model with a mid-mounted V8 engine. These two prototypes were manufactured and could be seen frequently on the roads around Maranello during that period, racking up plenty of test mileage. To date nothing further has developed from this project. It was carried out in conjunction with the Alcan Company of Canada, who provided a lightweight bonded aluminium chassis for the cars, which can be seen between them in this picture.

The 288 Evoluzione was the development vehicle for the upcoming F40 model and was based on the 288GTO, hence its name. A total of five examples were built, four of which were sold to private collectors, while this example, chassis number 79887, was retained by the factory. As can be seen, the general shape and styling details of the F40 are in place but further smoothing of the lines and alterations to the nose and rear wing profile would be carried out before the F40 was finally presented.

The F40 was presented to the world in Maranello in July 1987 and was a development, via the 288 Evoluzione, of the twin-turbo V8-engined 288GTO of 1984. The name F40 stands for Ferrari 40, to celebrate forty years of Ferrari car production. It was the last new model presented before the death of Enzo Ferrari, who was present at its unveiling, and it drew wide acclaim from the motoring press for its spectacular styling and shattering performance. The 3-litre twin-turbo V8 engine produced around 475bhp to provide lightning acceleration, and a claimed top speed of over 200mph. This was a racing car for the road and pushed road-car performance on to another plane. Limited series production ended in 1992, by which time a total of 1,311 examples had been produced, in both European and USA market versions.

From any angle the F40 looks powerful and purposeful and, like the limited production 288GTO, was produced in left-hand drive form only; you could have any colour you liked as long as you liked red. Initially it was standard procedure for owners to collect their car from the factory, where they were given instructions at the Fiorano circuit by factory test drivers in how to use the enormous power of the machine intelligently and safely.

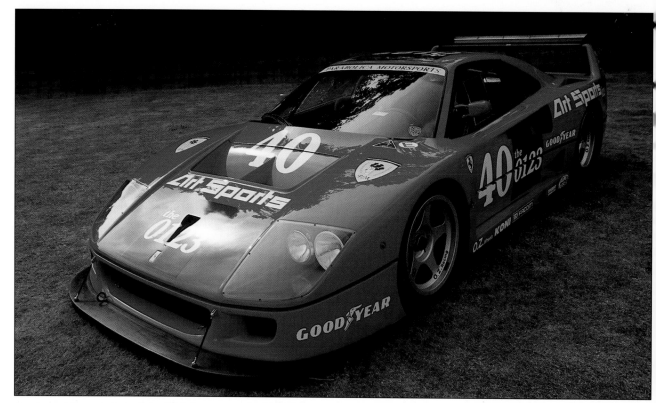

A competition version of the F40, known as the F40LM, was developed by Michelotto of Padova to contest the IMSA race series in the USA, which it did with a degree of success with the likes of Jean Alesi at the wheel. This racing effort was under the direction of the French concessionaire Ch. Pozzi Ferrari France. Subsequently these cars also raced at Le Mans, in Japan and in the BPR series in Europe.

When the F40LM showed promise in the European races a further development programme followed, resulting in the F40GT-E, seen here rounding the La Source hairpin at Spa-Francorchamps in 1996. They were always entered by private teams without factory support, which put them at a disadvantage against the factory backed entries of other makes. However, they were very quick and competitive and achieved a number of good results.

This is the first 348tb off the production line at Maranello, prior to the official launch of the model. The tape on the front left corner carries the number 1, although there were obviously prototypes before this car. The 348tb/ts models were the first series-production Ferraris to have a steel monocoque chassis instead of a tubular steel frame, a new departure in production technique for Ferrari. A new robotized body production line was installed at the Scaglietti works in Modena specifically to produce the shells for this model.

The 348tb, seen here with appropriate British registration plate, was announced in 1989 to replace the 328 series, along with the targa-roofed 348ts model. The t in the model title refers to the transverse gearbox arrangement that it shared with the Mondial t series, as it did also the mid-mounted longitudinal 3.4-litre V8 engine. In 1993 a special-edition model was produced for the American market in a series of one hundred cars and called the 348 Serie Speciale. The main visual differences were full body colour paintwork down to the base line, a small lip on the front spoiler and uncovered rear light assemblies.

This view of a 348ts model shows the Testarossa-like straked inlet ducts in the doors, feeding the side-mounted water radiators. Also evident are the aerodynamically foiled spokes of the wheels, still of the traditional Ferrari star pattern.

The 348 spider was announced at the 1993 Geneva Salon and concurrently on Rodeo Drive in Los Angeles, providing the first fully convertible two-seater Ferrari since the 365GTB/4S Daytona spider that went out of production twenty years previously. When erected, the hood echoed the cabin profile of the berlinetta variant. With the introduction of the spider version, the body colour paintwork was extended down to the base line, whereas 348tb/s models had a matt-black base strip around the complete perimeter of the car.

In the early 1990s Zagato offered this variation on the 348 theme, with heavily modified bodywork that included their trademark 'double-bubble' roof design, a Plexiglas engine cover, revised shape for the door radiator intakes, circular rear lights and a change of wheel design with split rims, together with the revised frontal treatment visible in this photograph.

In 1993 the model name was changed from 348tb/s to 348GTB/S. The only visual differences being the full body colour down to the base line and the revised tail badge with its upper case lettering. Towards the end of the production run in 1994 a limited-edition model of fifty examples was offered on the European market, called the 348GT Competizione. This model had kevlar-covered inner sill panels, special seats and steering wheel, while externally the identifying features were special split-rim wheels, enamel Scuderia Ferrari badges on the sides of the front wings and a 348GT Competizione tail badge.

A colourful array of 348 Challenge cars in the scrutineering area at Mugello in 1993, the final round in the first year of the Challenge race series.

The later sales brochures, those from the 1980s and '90s seen here, were more luxurious and usually larger than their earlier cousins.

Chapter 6

BUILDING FOR THE FUTURE

The 456GT was introduced in Brussels in September 1992 as part of the fortieth anniversary celebrations of the Belgian Ferrari importer, Garage Francorchamps. This was the 2+2 replacement for the 412 model that had ceased production in 1989. The new car stunned everybody with its smooth lines from the pen of Pininfarina, which had traces of the fabled Daytona around the rear quarters, but had a 2+2 seating arrangement within the compact cabin volume. It also had a reasonable boot space, particularly if the factory fitted space-optimising luggage was used. The all-new front-mounted V12 engine had a capacity of 5.5 litres, the 456 in the model title referring to the cubic capacity of a single cylinder, which was coupled to a six-speed transaxle. In 1996 a four-speed automatic transmission model was unveiled at the Geneva Salon which provided virtually identical performance to the manual model, with 0–60mph acceleration in 5.4 seconds and a top speed of around 185mph.

Introduction

From three cars in their first year of production just over fifty years ago, Ferrari now produce 3,500 road cars per year. They have the capacity to produce more and in fact did at the end of the 1980s when production peaked at over 4,000 cars. At that time the classic and collector car boom was at its peak and any Ferrari model had a queue of people eager to purchase it at almost any price. The crash in prices inevitably came and a sense of sanity returned to the market-place but the remaining market was saturated and Ferrari, like all the other exclusive car manufacturers, endured difficult times and, as is well known, some other companies did not survive. Fortunately, Ferrari have built up a hard-core loyal clientele over the years and with strong guidance from the company president, Luca Cordero Di Montezemolo, they weathered the storm with a resolve not to over-produce and to limit production to maintain the exclusivity and desirability of the product.

Hand in hand with this philosophy was a determination to update the range with the introduction of new models of increased quality, driveability and personality, while still maintaining the Ferrari charisma. The first result of this was the reintroduction of a 2+2 model, the 456GT, into the range in 1992, to which an automatic transmission option was subsequently added. Nearly six years after its introduction a minor facelift was presented at the 1998 Geneva Salon, when it became the 456GTM, a testament to the appropriateness of the original design. Whether this will be the last 2+2 Ferrari is difficult to say, as the situation vis-à-vis Maserati is thought to be that future 2+2 or four-seater models will come under their banner, with Ferrari models being exclusively two-seaters.

In 1993 Ferrari established two new initiatives to bring clients closer to the product and the factory. The first was the 'Pilota Ferrari' driving course aimed at providing clients with the opportunity to increase their driving skills and to maximize the potential of their Ferraris on a closed circuit under the guidance of experienced instructors. Over 1,200 clients have taken advantage of this scheme up to the end of 1997. The second was the introduction of a one-model race series, initially based on the 348 series and subsequently the F355, called the Ferrari Challenge. A special safety kit was offered to clients who wished to participate, with strict limitations on permitted modifications in the interests of mechanical equality. This has proved very popular and now consists of seven different series worldwide with the most successful participants in each group coming together at the end of the season for an inter-continental final.

The F355 model replaced the 348 in 1994 and was an instant success, the 3.5-litre, five-valve per cylinder engine offering one of the highest normally aspirated bhp/litre power outputs in the world. In 1997 the option of an Formula 1-style electro-hydraulically controlled steering-wheel paddle-actuated gear-change system was made available. This technological marvel offers the driver a choice of clutchless lightning-fast gear changes, or if desired it can be switched into automatic mode and used like an ordinary automatic gearbox – a clear case of racing improving the breed.

The F50 introduced at the Geneva Salon in 1995 was another case of Formula 1 technology being applied to a road car, this time in the form of its V12 Formula 1-derived engine and the carbon-fibre and composite materials used for its chassis and bodywork. With a limited production run of 349 cars (one less than Ferrari believed they could have sold) completed in 1997, Ferrari president, Luca Cordero Di Montezemolo, stated that this would be the last opportunity to build a car of this type owing to ever increasing legislative forces worldwide. However, the challenge of circumnavigating the rule book, or pushing it to its limits, is all part of the game for any company involved in motor racing.

Over two decades of a top of the range flat-twelve mid-engined two-seater model came to an end in 1996. The new 550 Maranello model was a return to a V12 configuration and the engine was mounted in front of the passenger compartment. Advances in tyre and suspension technology, particularly electronic control of the suspension under varying conditions, had enabled Ferrari to go against the conventional theory of the mid-engined layout providing optimum balance and roadholding. The new model not only had significantly better roadholding but also more power and the layout permitted a sensible luggage compartment, as well as a more refined and spacious interior.

When the 360 Modena replacement for the F355 was announced in early 1999, it could be seen that Ferrari had decided to maintain the mid-engine formula for their volume production V8 model series. However the ground effect principles of the F355 had been further extended, such that they dictated the 'face' of the car, of which the two prominent radiator grilles are the dominant feature. Some purists thought that it had lost its identity, but a large degree of the scepticism was withdrawn when the driving dynamics became apparent. A model to carry Ferrari through the opening years of the new century.

The latest offering from the Maranello stable, the 360 Modena, made its public debut at the 1999 Geneva Salon, as the replacement for the F355 model. It is obviously a completely different design philosophy from the pen of Pininfarina. One of the governing factors in the overall shape was aerodynamic efficiency which provided ground effect assistance to the roadholding.

From the rear the clean lines of the F355 berlinetta are evident, as are the large paired rear lights that are a return to a style popular on Ferraris during the 1970s and '80s. The clean shape also extends to the underside of the car, which is completely flat and incorporates twin venturi ducts to provide increased downforce at high speed.

For the first few months of F355 production the 348 Spider continued in production alongside the new model until its replacement, the F355 Spider, was announced in early 1995. The main advance with the F355 spider compared to its predecessor was the provision of electric operation of the folding hood, which is provided with a protective retaining cover when in the lowered position. In 1997 an Formula 1-style steering-column-mounted paddle gear change was made available as an option on the F355 range. This electo-hydraulically operated system provides a much faster gearchange than is possible with the standard manual lever and also gives the driver the facility of a fully automatic function should it be desired.

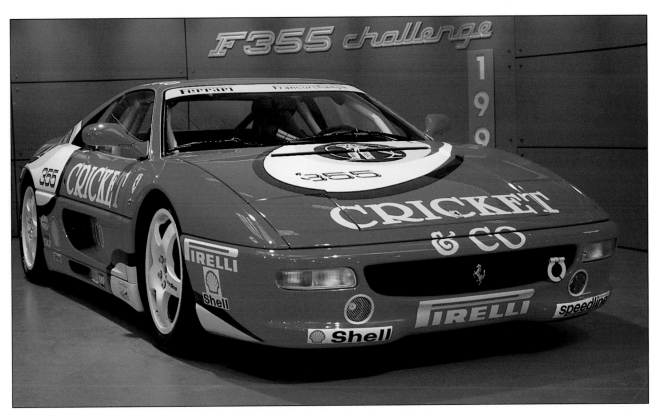

In 1993 Ferrari proposed a one-model race series for clients who wanted to use their 348 models in competition. They offered a safety kit to adapt the car for track use, which was obligatory, and was suitable for both 348tb and ts models. The series started in Europe but has since developed worldwide with regional groups that compete together in the final round of the year to find the Intercontinental champion. When the 348 model ceased production the series transferred to the F355 model, seen here in 1996 presentation specification at the Brussels Salon in January of that year.

During 1995 the series was open to both 348 and F355 models, providing a colourful spectacle of multi-hued variants, as seen in this picture of an F355 leading a 348 at Spa-Francorchamps, during the Spa Ferrari Days meeting in the May of that year. The 1998 regulations allow for the provision of a rear wing to the cars, otherwise they were virtually identical in appearance to the F355 seen leading here.

At the Geneva Salon in 1995 Ferrari presented another limited production, top of the performance league model which they called the F50, relating to fifty years since the foundation of the company. It has a longitudinally mid-mounted V12 engine derived from the 1990 Formula 1 car, with a capacity of 4.7 litres, mated to a six-speed gearbox which produces around 520bhp at 8500rpm. The complete chassis and body are constructed from carbon fibre, kevlar and nomex composite materials, making use of Formula 1 technology. A removable hardtop is provided, which is fitted to the example seen here.

In June 1996 the replacement for the mid-engined F512M was announced at a special meeting at the Nurburgring in Germany – the 550 Maranello. Advances in suspension technology has meant that a front-engined car can now handle and perform along with the best of the mid-engined examples. This configuration does not have the drawbacks of a mid-engined car, that is, a restricted cabin with noise from the engine immediately behind the occupants' heads and minimal practical luggage space. While similarities in overall line can be seen to the 456GT, the two-seater 550 Maranello has a much more aggressive frontal appearance reminiscent of an attacking shark when it appears in your rear-view mirror. The 5.5-litre V12 engine, mated to a six-speed transaxle, produces 485bhp at 7000rpm to give a factory quoted top speed of 199mph and a 0–60mph acceleration time of 4.3 seconds. These bear comparison with those of the F40 to show the advances in technology in a decade, from one model which was a lightly disguised racing car to the latest model which is a luxuriously appointed high-speed grand tourer, with plenty of luggage space and even room for a set of golf clubs.

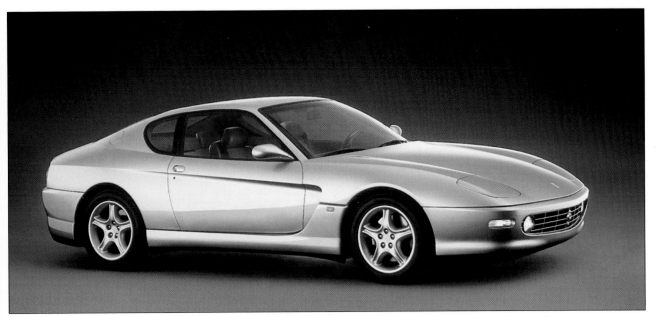

At the 1998 Geneva Salon a facelifted 456 model was presented with the suffix M for *modificato*, thus it became the 456M GT for the manual gearbox model and the 456M GTA for the version with the automatic gearbox. The main changes were to the interior which incorporated a revised dashboard and new seat designs, with the most obvious external changes being a revised front panel and radiator grille incorporating driving lights and the deletion of the exhaust vents on the bonnet behind the headlight pods.

The 360 Modena seen here at its Geneva show debut also breaks new ground in having an all aluminium chassis and body. It is powered by a longitudinally mid-mounted 3.6 litre V8 engine, which produces a claimed 400 bhp and gives a 180-plus mph top speed. Tradition is maintained at the rear with large twin rear light assemblies in a tail shape similar to the larger front engined 550 Maranello model.

Appendix

INTRODUCTION DATES OF
INDIVIDUAL MODELS

1947 125S, 159S, 166SC

1948 166 Sport Allemano coupé and spider,
166 Sport Touring coupé, 166 Inter
spider Corsa, 166MM barchetta

1949 166 Inter Touring coupé, 166 Inter
Farina coupé and spider, 166MM
Touring berlinetta

1950 166 Inter Vignale coupé, 166 Inter
Bertone cabriolet, 195 Sport Touring
berlinetta, 195 Inter Touring coupé,
195 Inter Ghia coupé, 195 Inter Motto
coupé, 195 Inter Vignale coupé, 275S
Touring barchetta

1951 212 Inter Ghia coupé, 195 and 212
Inter Ghia Aigle coupé, 212 Inter
Touring coupé, 212 Inter Farina coupé,
212 Inter Pinin Farina coupé and
cabriolet, 212 Inter Vignale coupé and
cabriolet, 212 Export Plus 340 America
Touring barchetta and berlinetta, 212
Export Vignale coupé, cabriolet and
spider, 212 Export Vignale coupé,
cabriolet and spider, 212 Export Motto
spider and berlinetta, 212 Export
Fontana spider and berlinetta, 240
America Vignale berlinetta

1952 212 Inter Ghia cabriolet, 225S Touring
barchetta, 225S Vignale spider and
berlinetta, 250S Vignale berlinetta, 240
Mexico Vignale spider and berlinetta,
340 America Vignale spider and coupé ,
342 America Vignale cabriolet, 342
America Pinin Farina coupé and
cabriolet

1953 166MM/53 Abarth spider, 166MM/53
Autodromo spider, 166MM/53 Vignale
spider and berlinetta, 166MM/53 Pinin
Farina berlinetta, 250 Europa Pinin
Farina coupé and cabriolet, 250 Europa
Vignale coupé, 250MM, 340MM and
375MM Pinin Farina berlinettas,
375MM Pinin Farina spider, 250MM
and 340MM Vignale spiders, 340MM
Touring spider, 375 America Pinin
Farina coupé, 375 America Vignale
coupé, 625TF Vignale spider and
coupé, 735S Autodromo spider

1954 250 Europa GT Pinin Farina coupé,
250 Europa GT Vignale coupé, 250
Monza Pinin Farina spider, 250 Monza
Scaglietti spider, 375MM Pinin Farina
coupé, 375MM Ghia coupé, 375 Plus
Pinin Farina spider and cabriolet, 375
Plus Sutton spider, 375 America
Vignale cabriolet, 500 Mondial Pinin
Farina spider and berlinetta, 750
Monza Pinin Farina spider, 500
Mondial and 750 Monza Scaglietti
spiders

1955 118LM, 121LM, 500 Mondial and
857S Monza Scaglietti spiders, 410
Superamerica S1 Pinin Farina coupé

1956 250GT Pinin Farina coupé-250GT
Boano coupé, 250GT LWB TDF Pinin
Farina berlinetta, 250GT LWB TDF
Zagato berlinetta, 250GT Pinin Farina
S1 cabriolet, 410SA S1 Ghia coupé,
410SA S1 Boano coupé and cabriolet,
625LM Touring spider, 290MM, 410S
and 500TR Scaglietti spiders

1957 250GT Ellena coupé, 250GT LWB
Pinin Farina California spider, 410SA

S2 Pinin Farina coupé, 410SA S2 Scaglietti coupé, 315S, 335S and 500TRC Scaglietti spiders

1958 250GT S1 Pininfarina coupé and cabriolet, 410SA S3 Pininfarina coupé, 250 Testa Rossa and 421 Monza Scaglietti spiders

1959 250GT LWB Interim berlinetta, 250GT SWB Pininfarina berlinetta, 250GT SWB Bertone berlinetta, 250GT S2 coupé and cabriolet, 410SA S3 Pininfarina coupé, 250 Testa Rossa '59 Fantuzzi spider

1960 250GT SWB California spider, 250GT SWB cabriolet Speciale, 250GTE 2+2, 400SA cabriolet and spider, 400 Superfast, 250 Testa Rossa Fantuzzi spider

1961 250GT SWB Bertone berlinetta, 400SA coupé Pininfarina Aerodinamico S1, 250TRI '61 Fantuzzi spider

1962 250GTO berlinetta, 250GT Lusso berlinetta, 400SA coupé Pininfarina Aerodinamica S2, 400SA S2 cabriolet

1963 330 America 2+2 coupé, 330LM berlinetta, 330GT 2+2 S1 coupé, 250LM berlinetta

1964 250GTO '64 berlinetta, 275 GTB berlinetta, 275 GTS spider, 500 Superfast S1 coupé

1965 275 GTB/C berlinetta, 330GT 2+2 S2 coupé, 500 Superfast S2 coupé

1966 330 GTC coupé, 330 GTS spider, 365 California spider, 275 GTB/4 berlinetta

1967 275 GTB/4 NART spider, 365GT 2+2 coupé

1968 Dino 206 GT coupé, 365 GTB/4 Daytona coupé, 365 GTC coupé, 365 GTS spider

1969 246 GT coupé, 365 GTS spider, 365 GTS/4 Daytona spider

1971 365 GTC/4 coupé, 365 GTB/4C coupé

1972 246 GTS spider, 365 GT4 2+2 coupé

1973 365 GT4 berlinetta boxer

1974 Dino 308 GT4 2+2 coupé

1975 Dino 208 GT4 2+2 coupé

1976 308 GTB, 512BB, 400GT and 400GT/A 2+2 coupé

1977 308 GTS

1979 400i and 400i/A 2+2 coupé

1980 Mondial 8 2+2 coupé, 208 GTB/GTS, 308GTBi/GTSi

1981 512BBi

1982 Mondial QV 2+2 coupé, 308 GTB/S QV, 208 GTB turbo

1983 208 GTS Turbo, Mondial QV 2+2 cabriolet

1984 288 GTO, Testarossa

1985 Mondial 3.2 2+2 coupé and cabriolet, 328 GTB/S, 421 2+2 coupé

1986 GTB/S Turbo

1987 F40

1989 348 tb/s, Mondial t 2+2 coupé and cabriolet

1992 512 TR, 456GT 2+2 coupé

1993 348 spider, 348GTB/S, 348 Serie Speciale

1994 348 GT Competizione, F355 GTB/S, F512M

1995 F355 spider, F50

1996 456 GTA 2+2 coupé, 550 Maranello berlinetta

1997 F355 GTB/S and spider Formula 1

1998 456GTM and GTM/A 2+2 coupé

1999 360 Modena

INDEX